JESUS LINK

A Bible Trivia Challenge

ELLEN CAUGHEY

BARBOUR BOOKS
An Imprint of Barbour Publishing, Inc.

JESUS
LINK

© 2002 by Barbour Publishing, Inc.

ISBN 1-58660-497-X

Published by Barbour Books, an imprint of Barbour Publishing, Inc., P.O. Box 719, Uhrichsville, Ohio 44683
www.barbourbooks.com

ecpa Member of the
Evangelical Christian
Publishers Association

Printed in the United States of America.

CONTENTS

INTRODUCTION

Welcome to *Jesus Link*. Contestants, you're looking pretty sure of yourselves. Ah, yes, there's that familiar smile before beginning your litany of Sunday school success stories. There's that twinkle in the eye that begs for a pair of Ray-Bans.

A faithful attendee of church since infancy? Oh, and let's not forget all those Vacation Bible Schools where you likely won annual honors for perfect attendance.

Not to burst your bubble, but it's my guess you've just crossed the Jordan and landed on alien quiz-game territory. Will you cave in like the ten frightened spies, or, like Joshua and Caleb, stick around and give it your best shot? Many are called but few succeed at playing *Jesus Link!*

What follows are thirty names or descriptions of Jesus Christ, the Son of God. Each name will be the subject of intense scrutiny, in the form of twenty questions from relatively elementary to downright demanding. (Keep in mind that Scripture quotations used in the questions are taken from the New International Version of the Bible, unless otherwise noted.)

All questions for each round are assigned equal point value, with that value increasing from round to round. Points won will carry over from one round to the next, with the grand total given at the end of the final round. If you want to win, you'll have to work for it.

Time to prove your mettle. Round 1 is waiting.

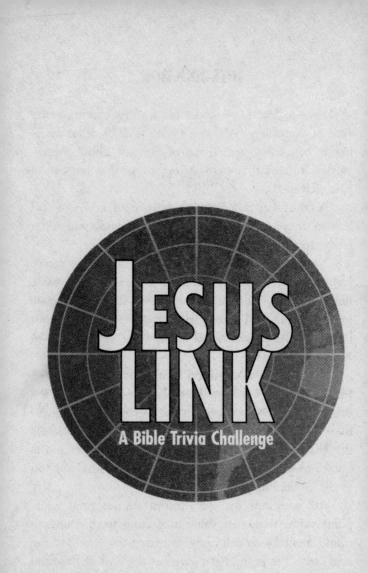

JESUS LINK

A Bible Trivia Challenge

Round 1:
JESUS

How do we begin to make the *Jesus Link*? By connecting with the only source of absolute truth, the Bible, God's Holy Word. Every name or description of Jesus has its root in Scripture; every name, therefore, is a link to the true character of the one and only Son of God.

The first name, appropriately, is *Jesus*. Scripture says, "Thou shalt call his name JESUS: for he shall save his people from their sins" (Matthew 1:21 KJV). No matter who you are, you cannot save yourself. And that's good—because you are several box tops short of a free lunch box.

It's time to play. . .*Jesus Link!*

ROUND 1:
JESUS

Each question in Round 1 is worth 5 points.
Total number of points in this round: 100

1. *Jesus* is the Greek form of what Hebrew name that means "the Lord saves"?

2. While Mary, Jesus' mother, could trace her family tree back to King David, to what king of Israel could Jesus' legal and earthly father, Joseph, trace his lineage?

3. Besides Jesus, name one earthly "brother" of His who was a biological son of Mary and Joseph.

4. When Jesus first began to preach, he used the phrase "the kingdom of heaven" as opposed to "the kingdom of God" so as not to offend whom?

5. Where did Jesus perform His first miracle?

6. In Jesus' "Sermon on the Mount," who are those who will see God?

7. Instead of "eye for eye, and tooth for tooth," Jesus said that we are to show love toward whom?

8. Of whom did Jesus say, "I tell you the truth, I have not found anyone in Israel with such great faith"?

9. What disciple's mother-in-law did Jesus heal of a fever?

10. Jesus told His disciples that they must be as innocent as doves and as shrewd as what creatures?

11. To whom did Jesus send this message? "The blind receive sight, the lame walk, those who have leprosy are cured, the deaf hear, the dead are raised, and the good news is preached to the poor."

12. Besides those of Korazin, the citizens of what other two cities are cited by Jesus as refusing to repent of their sins and believe in Him?

13. On two occasions, Jesus is recorded as feeding crowds numbering in the thousands. How many were in each crowd?

14. While seven is considered the perfect number, Jesus tells Peter that we should forgive those who offend us not seven but this many times.

15. Of the "seven last words" of Jesus on the cross, what is considered the seventh?

To whom did Jesus first appear following His resurrection?

 Following that appearance, Jesus joins two men on their way to what village?

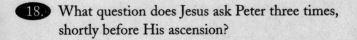 What question does Jesus ask Peter three times, shortly before His ascension?

 What things did Jesus say make a person unclean?

20. Jesus said, "Heaven and earth will pass away. . ." but what two-word answer would not?

ANSWER KEY/ROUND 1: JESUS

1. Joshua
2. King David (see Matthew 1)
3. James, Joses, Judas, or Simon
4. The Jews
5. Cana (see John 2)
6. The pure in heart (Matthew 5:8)
7. Our enemies (Matthew 5:44)
8. The Roman centurion whose servant lay paralyzed at home (Matthew 8:10)
9. Peter (Matthew 8:14–15)
10. Snakes or serpents (Matthew 10:16)
11. John the Baptist, who was in prison (Matthew 11:4)
12. Capernaum and Bethsaida (Matthew 11:21–23)
13. 5,000 and 4,000 (Matthew 14:13ff.; 15:32ff.)
14. 77 times (Matthew 18:22) or 70 times 7 (KJV)
15. "Father, into your hands I commit my spirit" (Luke 23:46)
16. Mary Magdalene and Mary the mother of James and Joses
17. Emmaus (Luke 24:13)
18. "Do you love me?" (John 21:15ff.)
19. The things that come out of the mouth, that come from the heart (Matthew 15:11)
20. "My words" (Matthew 24:35)

YOUR SCORE: _____
(out of a possible 100 points)

ROUND 1: JESUS/WRAP-UP

Are you still likely to be confused with a brain surgeon? Or can you now admit that your knowledge of Jesus is sorely lacking?

Jesus, the Son of God, wants you to know Him as you've known no one else. He doesn't want to be only the stuff of Sunday school recitation. No, Jesus wants His words to become heart knowledge. He wants to have a true relationship with you; He wants to be your Friend.

To see God one day in heaven, to be pure in heart, we must accept Jesus first. Only then can we truly love our enemies; only then can we believe by faith alone that Jesus will do what He says.

So far, we know Jesus was a miracle worker and a preacher with a radically different message who was crucified and came back to life three days later. Yet the words He spoke so persistently to Peter make one pause. "Do you love me?" Jesus asks each one of us, just as He asked the disciple who once denied Him three times. The way we answer that question determines the rest of our lives— and beyond.

Time to move on. Round 2 beckons.

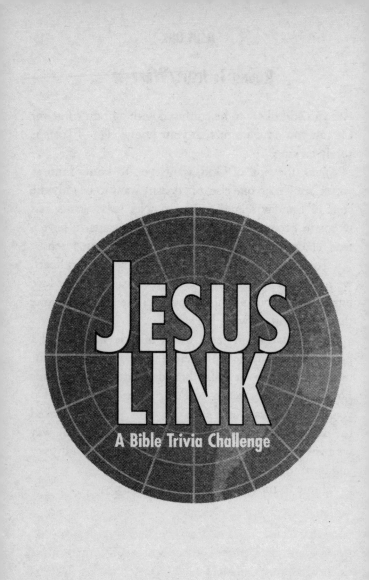

JESUS LINK

A Bible Trivia Challenge

ROUND 2:
CREATOR

Round 2, and we are taking baby steps. If you feel a modicum of pride? satisfaction? relief? after the first inquisition, rest assured those emotions will be replaced by the more familiar frustration, despair, and self-loathing in the very near future (wink).

We are about to meet Jesus the *Creator*, a title you may not at first associate with the Son of God. But indeed He was, as Scripture acknowledges: "He is the image of the invisible God, the firstborn over all creation. For by him all things were created: things in heaven and on earth, visible and invisible, whether thrones or powers or rulers or authorities; all things were created by him and for him. He is before all things, and in him all things hold together" (Colossians 1:15–17).

Jesus came to save that which He created. And that's good news for you, since you are a couple lutzes short of a bronze medal.

It's time to play. . . *Jesus Link!*

Round 2:
Creator

Each question in Round 2 is worth 6 points.
Total number of points in this round: 120

1. When does Scripture say that Jesus was chosen to come to earth and offer a sacrifice for our sins?

2. Paul says you should "put on the new self," renewed in the knowledge that you were created in the image of whom?

3. Daniel refers to Jesus as the "Ancient of _____"?

4. Like Daniel, in the Book of Revelation John describes Jesus as having hair of what color?

Who are the foundations of "God's house-hold," according to Paul, and who is its chief cornerstone?

Complete this sentence from Matthew describing Jesus: "I will open my mouth in parables, I will utter things hidden since _____."

What two *W* words did Jesus' disciples utter when they said, "Who is this? Even the _____ and the _____ obey him"?

 After Jesus spoke about His impending death for the second time, the disciples began arguing among themselves. What was the gist of their dispute?

To His quibbling disciples, Jesus, the Creator and Son of God, describes Himself as what?

10. The one whom God esteems, according to the prophet Isaiah, possesses first what quality beginning with the letter *H?*

11. If heaven is the Creator's throne, what is His footstool, according to Isaiah?

12. From Isaiah to the books of 2 Peter and Revelation, much is revealed about the new heaven and new earth that will exist after Jesus' second coming. What city will be known as the Holy City?

13. In the Holy City, what sound, according to Isaiah, will be heard no more?

14. According to the Creator, what two animals will feed together in the new heaven on earth?

15. While the world was created the first time "out of water and by water," according to Peter, the present world will be destroyed by what means?

16. Seated on the throne in the Book of Revelation, Jesus tells the disciple John, "I am making everything____!"

17. What is the second death?

18. What geometric shape will the new Holy City have?

19. How thick will the walls of the Holy City be?

20. Without a sun or moon, what will provide light in the Holy City?

ANSWER KEY/ROUND 2: CREATOR

1. "Before the creation of the world" (1 Peter 1:20)
2. Your Creator, Jesus Christ (Colossians 3:10)
3. "The Ancient of Days" (Daniel 7:13)
4. White (as wool and snow) (Revelation 1:14)
5. The foundation is the apostles and prophets; the chief cornerstone is Christ Jesus (Ephesians 2:19–20)
6. "The creation of the world" (Matthew 13:35, referring to Psalm 78:2)
7. Wind, waves (Mark 4:41)
8. Who would be the greatest in Jesus' kingdom on earth (Mark 9:33–34)
9. A servant (Luke 22:27)
10. Humility (Isaiah 66:2)
11. The earth (Isaiah 66:1)
12. Jerusalem (Revelation 21)
13. The sound of weeping and crying (Isaiah 65:19)
14. The wolf and the lamb (Isaiah 65:25)
15. By fire (2 Peter 3:7)
16. "I am making everything new!" (Revelation 21:5)
17. The final end for unbelievers, described as a fiery lake of burning sulfur (Revelation 21:8)
18. That of a square (Revelation 21:16)
19. 144 cubits (Revelation 21:17)
20. The glory of God and/or the lamb (Revelation 21:23)

YOUR SCORE: _____
(out of a possible 120 points)
Total number of points from both rounds: _____
Total possible points: 220

ROUND 2: CREATOR/WRAP-UP

Even though Jesus presented Himself on earth as a servant and not as the firstborn of creation, a probing of the Scriptures reveals a more complete picture of the Son of God. Jesus was not only the *Creator* of the world as we know it, but He will be the Creator of the new heaven on earth sometime in the future. The question for now is, how can we reconcile both sides of Jesus in our Christian lives?

As Christians, we should be humble and without pride, with all personal ambition directed toward furthering the kingdom of God. We serve an omnipotent Creator, One whom we can trust completely, and One with whom we will one day reside in unbelievable splendor. We can accomplish nothing on our own—but everything in Jesus' name!

And, as Christians, we should look forward each day to Jesus' coming. As Paul writes, "Therefore you do not lack any spiritual gift as you eagerly wait for our Lord Jesus Christ to be revealed. He will keep you strong to the end, so that you will be blameless on the day of our Lord Jesus Christ" (1 Corinthians 1:7–8).

Time to dust off the sandals and pick up the walking stick. Round 3 is no mirage.

ROUND 3:
ROOT OF JESSE

Round 3, and we plod on. So far you've managed to score a most impressive _____ number of points (wink). Perhaps you've been waiting for your chance to delve into ancient history, undoubtedly a forte of all Sunday school valedictorians. Time to seize the opportunity!

Long before Jesus was born on earth, He was destined to fulfill many Old Testament prophecies. Among these was Isaiah's declaration, "And in that day there shall be a root of Jesse. . .to it shall the Gentiles seek: and his rest shall be glorious" (Isaiah 11:10 KJV). This blessing to both Jews and Gentiles was partially fulfilled with Jesus' birth and will be most completely realized with His second coming.

Ready to piece together the shards of the archaeological dig that is otherwise known as your memory? Thankfully, we can trust God's Word to fill in the gaping holes and illuminate those dimly lit passageways.

It's time to play. . .*Jesus Link!*

ROUND 3:
ROOT OF JESSE

Each question in Round 3 is worth 7 points.
Total number of points in this round: 140

 1. In what town did Jesse live?

 2. How many sons did Jesse have?

 3. Of these sons of Jesse, who was the oldest and who was the youngest?

 4. Which son of Jesse would succeed Saul as king?

 5. What prophet delivered this message from God to David: "Your house and your kingdom will endure forever before me; your throne will be established forever"?

6. From what Old Testament book was Peter quoting when he said in the Book of Acts, " 'Because you will not abandon me to the grave, nor will you let your Holy One see decay. You have made known to me the paths of life; you will fill me with joy in your presence' "?

7. Prior to listing the genealogy of Jesus, Matthew calls Jesus not only the son of David but also the son of what Old Testament patriarch?

8. Who was David's great-grandmother?

9. What same number of generations occurred from Abraham to David, from David to the Babylonian captivity, and from the captivity to the birth of Jesus?

10. "The Lord God will give him the throne of his father David. . . ." Who delivered this message to Jesus' earthly mother, Mary?

Only Matthew records Jesus' first encounter with two blind men. What do they call Jesus?

 When Jesus is criticized by the Pharisees for picking and eating grain on the Sabbath, whom from the Old Testament did Jesus cite as having also satisfied his hunger in violation of the law?

 What *S* word completes Jesus' sentence: "I desire mercy, not _____."

 Who was David's grandfather?

 What Jericho woman with a shady reputation was blessed because of her obedience to God with a place in Jesus' family tree?

 On what holy hill does David write in Psalms that God will "install my King"?

17. When Jesus cried on the cross, "My God, my God, why have you forsaken me," He was repeating a line from what Old Testament book?

18. When David writes, "They divide my garments among them and cast lots for my clothing," to what is he referring?

19. On what occasion did David utter these words: "When one rules over men in righteousness, when he rules in the fear of God, he is like the light of morning at sunrise. . ."?

20. While David was anointed with oil by the prophet Samuel, the writer of Hebrews says that God has anointed Jesus with the oil of what?

Answer Key/Round 3: Root of Jesse

1. Bethlehem (1 Samuel 16:1)
2. Eight sons (1 Samuel 16)
3. Eliab was the oldest (1 Samuel 17:13); David was the youngest (1 Samuel 16:11)
4. David (1 Samuel 16:13)
5. Nathan (2 Samuel 7:16)
6. The Book of Psalms (Acts 2:27–28; Psalm 16:10–11)
7. Abraham (Matthew 1:1)
8. Ruth (Matthew 1:5)
9. Fourteen generations (Matthew 1:17)
10. The angel Gabriel (Luke 1:26, 32)
11. Son of David (Matthew 9:27)
12. David (Matthew 12:3)
13. Sacrifice (Matthew 12:7)
14. Obed (Matthew 1:5)
15. Rahab the prostitute (Matthew 1:5)
16. On Zion (seePsalm 2:6)
17. The Psalms (see Psalm 22:1)
18. Jesus would suffer this fate during His crucifixion (Psalm 22:18; Matthew 27:35)
19. On his deathbed (2 Samuel 23:3–4)
20. The oil of joy (Hebrews 1:9)

Your score: _____
(out of a possible 140 points)
Total number of points from all rounds: _____
Total possible points: 360

ROUND 3: ROOT OF JESSE/WRAP-UP

It's hard work rooting about among the ruins, isn't it? Time to put down your pick and shovel and think about what you've uncovered—and we've only begun to reveal the legion of prophecies that foretold the arrival of Jesus!

How can so many doubt Jesus when King David and others have written all those psalms about Him? Who else could have fulfilled every one of those prophecies? The answer, of course, is no one. From His birth to His crucifixion and resurrection, every event was specifically prophesied hundreds of years earlier.

God promised to send His Son, One who would fulfill all that was written about Him. We know from the writer of Hebrews that "it is impossible for God to lie" (Hebrews 6:18). As we proceed, the evidence will become too great to ignore. Jesus, the *Root of Jesse* and of the royal line of King David, is the only Son of God.

Do you have the courage to continue making the *Jesus Link*? Round 4 is not for the cobweb-challenged.

ROUND 4:
WONDERFUL COUNSELOR

Are you still busy cleaning out the dusty attic of your once-proficient memory? Or are the lights on and nobody's home? Let's face it: Everyone could use some help around the house.

Just in time we meet Jesus, the *Wonderful Counselor*, a name given Him once again by the prophet Isaiah: "For to us a child is born, to us a son is given, and the government will be on his shoulders. And he will be called Wonderful Counselor. . ." (Isaiah 9:6).

What are the attributes of a counselor? Surely one of the most important is to offer guidance and lead the way to a better life. Hang on to these questions, team—because you are several oars short of a catamaran.

It's time to play. . *Jesus Link!*

ROUND 4:
WONDERFUL COUNSELOR

Each question in Round 4 is worth 8 points.
Total number of points in this round: 160

 1. Whom did Jesus advise, "No one can see the kingdom of God unless he is born again"?

 2. Where did Jesus encounter a woman at a well?

3. Although Jesus asked the woman for water to drink, what kind of water did He offer to give her?

 4. According to Jesus, how can one cross over from death to life?

5. When the Pharisees brought a woman to Jesus who was caught committing adultery, what did Jesus do first?

6. Complete this sentence. Jesus advised the Pharisees, "If any one of you is without sin, _____."

7. To the Jews who believed in Him, Jesus said, "Then you will know the truth, and the truth _____." Complete the sentence.

8. What did certain Jews call Jesus after He proclaimed, "If anyone keeps my word, he will never see death"?

9. According to Jesus, all men will know that you are His disciple if you do what?

10. Who is the Counselor that Jesus says He will ask the Father to give His followers?

What will the Counselor, who will live with you, teach you?

 Fill in the blank. Jesus also calls the Counselor the Spirit of _____.

 The Counselor will "speak only _____, and he will tell you what is yet to come." Complete this sentence.

 On what occasion did the Holy Spirit come upon the disciples?

 How many days following what Jewish holiday did this occur?

 How many days following Jesus' ascension did this occasion occur?

 What was the first immediate effect on Jesus' disciples upon receiving the Holy Spirit?

18. Speaking of the future, Jesus tells of wars, earthquakes, and famines that are to come. By standing firm, He says, we will gain _____.

19. We will know that the kingdom of God is near, Jesus says, speaking in a parable, when what kind of tree sprouts leaves?

20. What is the Great Commission that Jesus gives His disciples before being taken up to heaven?

Answer Key/Round 4: Wonderful Counselor

1. Nicodemus (John 3:1–3)
2. Samaria (John 4)
3. Water "welling up to eternal life" (John 4:14)
4. By hearing His Word and believing in Him who sent Jesus, one can receive eternal life (John 5:24)
5. He bent down and started writing on the ground with His finger (John 8:6)
6. ". . .let him be the first to throw a stone at her" (John 8:7)
7. ". . .will set you free" (John 8:32)
8. Demon-possessed (John 8:52)
9. Love one another (John 13:35)
10. The Holy Spirit—the Spirit of God or Jesus Himself (John 14:16)
11. All things (John 14:26)
12. Truth (John 16:13)
13. "what he hears" (John 16:13)
14. The day of Pentecost (Acts 2:1)
15. 50 days after Passover
16. 10 days after the ascension
17. They began to speak in different languages (tongues) (Acts 2:4)
18. Life (Luke 21:19)
19. A fig tree (Luke 21:29)
20. "Go into all the world and preach the good news to all creation" (Mark 16:15)

Your score: _____
(out of a possible 160 points)
Total number of points from all rounds: _____
Total possible points: 520

Round 4: Wonderful Counselor/Wrap-up

Psalm 73 proclaims the hope embodied in Jesus' resurrection: "You guide me with your counsel, and afterward you will take me into glory" (verse 24). While He walked the earth, Jesus counseled many, with His words preserved to guide every generation since. But His role as Counselor didn't end there.

From our review of Scripture, we know Jesus provided another Counselor, the Holy Spirit, to give us His words and direction when He could no longer be in the flesh with us. The Holy Spirit *is* Jesus with us—but only if we first believe that He is the Son of God.

Before moving on, two Old Testament verses come to mind concerning this *Wonderful Counselor*. The words of Proverbs 3:6 are familiar yet so true: "In all your ways acknowledge him, and he will make your paths straight." And then there is the simply stated position of King Jehoshaphat: "First seek the counsel of the LORD" (1 Kings 22:5).

Time to hit the trail, team. Round 5 is just around the bend.

ROUND 5:
EVERLASTING FATHER

Are you still polishing your acceptance speech for the Nobel Prize? Still harboring illusions of thanking the Academy?

I may be off the mark, but at this point in the game I believe you're ready for the comforts of home, and to be in the company of One who knows and loves you better than anyone. Only an *Everlasting Father* can hold you in His arms and never let you go.

Once again, we find the source for this name of Jesus in Isaiah: "He will be called. . .Everlasting Father" (Isaiah 9:6). Jesus as Father embodies the best of a loving parent because you are the work of His hand and so precious to Him.

It's time to play. . .*Jesus Link!*

ROUND 5:
EVERLASTING FATHER

Each question in Round 5 is worth 9 points.
Total number of points in this round: 180

 1. From what Old Testament book (or scroll) does Jesus read the following when He returns to a Nazareth synagogue for the Sabbath? "He has anointed me to preach good news to the poor. . . to release the oppressed. . . ."

 2. What *M* word spoken by Jesus fills in these blanks? "Be ____, just as your Father is ____."

3. In what town did Jesus encounter a widow who had lost her only son?

4. Filled with compassion, Jesus performs what miracle during the funeral procession for the widow's son?

Whose child did Jesus, before bringing her back to life, describe as follows? "She is not dead but asleep."

 Complete this sentence: "Whoever welcomes this little child in my name welcomes ___."

7. In the Parable of the Good Samaritan, what two men pass by the wounded man without stopping to help him?

 Complete this sentence spoken by Jesus of the Samaritan who was a good neighbor: "Go and do _____."

9. In what parable does Jesus quote, " 'My son, . . . you are always with me, and everything I have is yours' "?

10. Jesus said, "I praise you, Father, . . .because you have hidden these things from the wise and learned, and revealed them to little children." Who are the "little children" of whom Jesus is speaking?

11. What *Y* word does Jesus use in the following passage? "Come to me, all you who are weary and burdened, . . .for my _____ is easy and my burden is light."

12. Paul writes that we did not receive a spirit that makes us a slave to fear but rather, the Spirit of _____. Fill in the blank.

13. Complete this sentence. "We are more than _____," Paul writes, "through him who loved us."

Complete this sentence by the writer of Hebrews: "The Lord disciplines those he loves, and he punishes everyone he accepts as a _____."

15. Paul writes in 2 Corinthians that we praise a Father of compassion and the God of all _____. Fill in the blank.

16. John writes that we are children of God, and the whole world is under the control of whom?

17. What is the Aramaic word for "daddy"?

18. Fill in the blank. Jesus tells us that in His Father's house are many _____.

19. Only Jesus has seen the _____, since He is from God. Fill in the blank.

20. The shortest verse in the Bible, "Jesus wept," occurs during the telling of what story?

Answer Key/Round 5: Everlasting Father

1. The Book of Isaiah (Luke 4:17–18)
2. Merciful (Luke 6:36)
3. A town called Nain (Luke 7:11)
4. He brought him back to life (Luke 7:14–15)
5. The daughter of Jairus (Luke 8:51–52)
6. Me (Luke 9:48)
7. A priest and a Levite (Luke 10:31–32)
8. Likewise (Luke 10:37)
9. The Parable of the Lost or Prodigal Son (Luke 15:11ff.)
10. Those who are humble and open to receive and understand God's Word (Luke 10:21)
11. Yoke (Matthew 11:28, 30)
12. Sonship (Romans 8:15)
13. Conquerors (Romans 8:37)
14. Son (Hebrews 12:6)
15. Comfort (2 Corinthians 1:3)
16. The evil one (1 John 5:19)
17. "Abba" (see Romans 8:15)
18. Rooms or mansions (John 14:2)
19. Father (John 6:46)
20. The raising of Lazarus from the dead (John 11:35)

Your score: _____
(out of a possible 180 points)
Total number of points from all rounds: _____
Total possible points: 700

Round 5: Everlasting Father/Wrap-up

"The eternal God is your refuge," we read in Deuteronomy 33:27, "and underneath are the everlasting arms." What a picture of our *Everlasting Father!*

If we believe that Jesus is the Son of God, we have the privilege to become children—sons and daughters—of our heavenly Father. From that moment on, we have the incalculable gift of His love and compassion. We have the assurance that we can take any problem or concern to Him, and He will give us the necessary peace and strength to continue living purposefully. And, if we simply have faith in Him, we have the promise of eternal life spent with our wonderful Father.

Have you heard His voice of calm penetrating the inky darkness? Have you felt His joy when you thought life couldn't be any better? Can you call Him "Abba"?

Time to leave the feathered nest. Round 6 will be a wake-up call.

ROUND 6:
PRINCE OF PEACE

Round 6, and the spring in our step is all too visible. Time to raise the bar, or in your case, stay the course.

Time to enter into the presence of royalty and become acquainted with the first of Jesus' many titles. We know already that Jesus was born into the royal line of King David, who ruled over Israel and waged war against many enemies on behalf of his country. This title, *Prince of Peace*, is not limited to geography or time. Jesus' life on earth, His ministry, and His reign to come provide ample evidence that He is most deserving of such an accolade. Indeed, He is the only source of true peace.

Once again, we turn to Isaiah 9:6 for verification: "For to us a child is born, to us a son is given. . .and he will be called. . .Prince of Peace."

Time to stop waging war with your memory. It's time to play. . *Jesus Link!*

ROUND 6:
PRINCE OF PEACE

Each question in Round 6 is worth 10 points.
Total number of points in this round: 200

 1. When John the Baptist baptized Jesus, what descended from above onto Jesus?

 2. Whom did Jesus call the "sons of God" in His "Sermon on the Mount"?

3. Instead of suing your enemy and taking him to court, what course of action did Jesus advise?

4. What is Jesus' one allowance for divorce?

5. Jesus' admonition to turn the other cheek and go the extra mile was in reaction to what Old Testament law found in three books of Moses?

6. "Do not suppose that I have come to bring peace to the earth," Jesus said. What did He mean?

7. Complete this sentence. Aware that His time to die was not at hand, Jesus withdrew from the synagogue and the Pharisees to fulfill this prophecy from the Old Testament: "A bruised _____ he will not break."

8. Whom does Jesus call the "prince of this world"?

9. "Peace I leave with you; my peace I give you." To what peace was Jesus referring?

10. "I have told you these things, so that in me you may have peace," Jesus said to His disciples shortly before His betrayal and death. To what things was Jesus referring?

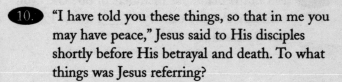

What is the first thing Jesus says to His disciples—in fact, He says it twice—when they are all together following His resurrection?

 Complete this sentence. "We have peace with God through our Lord Jesus Christ," Paul writes to the church at Rome, "through whom we have gained access by faith into this _____."

13. Fill in the blank. The peace of God, writes Paul to the church at Philippi, transcends all _____.

14. Instead of being anxious, we should _____, advises Paul. Fill in the blank.

15. Fill in the blank. As members of one body (of believers), we are called to ____, writes Paul to the Colossians.

16. With what are we to "clothe" ourselves, according to Paul, to achieve perfect unity as believers of Jesus? Name three out of five characteristics.

Which of the seven seals the Lamb opens in the Book of Revelation contains the horse and rider who has the power to take peace from the earth?

 The leaves of the tree of life in the new heaven on earth will be used for what purpose?

19. Fill in the blank. Luke writes that when we see signs of the end times take place, we are to rejoice because our _____ is "drawing near."

20. "Consider the blameless, observe the upright," writes David the psalmist, "there is a future for the man of _____." Complete the sentence.

ANSWER KEY/ROUND 6: PRINCE OF PEACE

1. A dove (Matthew 3:16)
2. The peacemakers (Matthew 5:9)
3. Settling matters out of court (Matthew 5:25)
4. Marital unfaithfulness (Matthew 5:32)
5. "Eye for eye, and tooth for tooth" (Matthew 5:38)
6. Jesus brings a lasting peace for all for the past, present, and future, and not a temporary peace to fix present difficulties (see Matthew 10:34ff.)
7. A bruised reed (Isaiah 42:1–4; Matthew 12:20)
8. Satan, or the evil one (John 16:11)
9. The peace conveyed by the Holy Spirit (John 14:27)
10. That the disciples would be scattered but that He would be with His Father (God) (John 16:33)
11. "Peace be with you!" (John 20:19)
12. "Grace in which we now stand" (Romans 5:1–2)
13. Understanding (Philippians 4:7)
14. Pray (Philippians 4:6)
15. Peace (Colossians 3:15)
16. Compassion, kindness, humility, gentleness, and patience (Colossians 3:12)
17. The second seal (Revelation 6:3–4)
18. The healing of nations (Revelation 22:2)
19. Redemption (Luke 21:28)
20. Peace (Psalm 37:37)

YOUR SCORE: _____
(out of a possible 200 points)
Total number of points from all rounds: _____
Total possible points: 900

ROUND 6: PRINCE OF PEACE/WRAP-UP

From the Gospel accounts, we have clear evidence of the peaceful stands Jesus took while He walked the earth. To cite a few examples, we should love our neighbors, pray for our enemies, settle disputes out of court, and strive for harmony in marriage.

Jesus as an advocate for peace was further underscored following His resurrection through His apostle Paul. Indeed, as believers of Jesus Christ, Paul writes, we are committed to peace and to daily prayer to achieve that objective. As the time for Jesus' return becomes more imminent—that is, with each passing day—we should rejoice and be glad. Only then will ultimate and lasting peace be achieved.

Hundreds of years before Jesus' birth, Isaiah wrote, "In his law the islands will put their hope" (Isaiah 42:4). That name is *Prince of Peace*.

The incredible but true journey continues. Team, prepare to depart for Round 7.

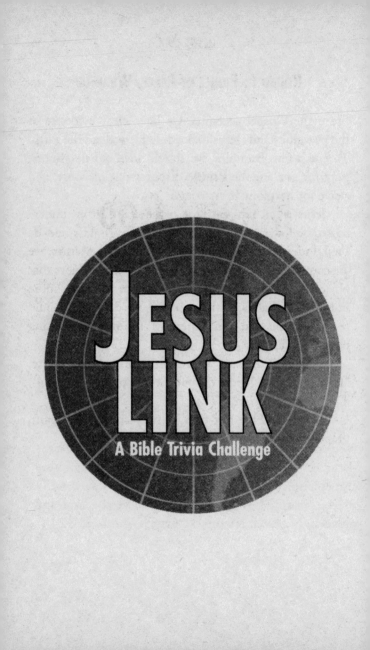

JESUS LINK

A Bible Trivia Challenge

ROUND 7:
MIGHTY GOD

Have all these questions left you reeling? Before you're tempted to push the C(lear) button of your brain, stop to consider this name of Jesus: *Mighty God*.

Maybe this appellation will still compute. Yes, there in the recesses of your memory is the faint glimmer of recognition. Eureka! There's that Sunday school lesson smothered with sticky gold stars, several of which ended up on your forehead. The name was first given in Isaiah 9:6—"To us a son is given. . .and he will be called. . . Mighty God"—but its power was clearly evident hundreds of years later. Paul writes, "I can do everything through him who gives me strength" (Philippians 4:13).

Get ready, bantamweights, to meet the one and only Mighty God. It's time to play. . .*Jesus Link!*

ROUND 7:
MIGHTY GOD

Each question in Round 7 is worth 11 points.
Total number of points in this round: 220

 1. In the middle of a fierce storm, what did Jesus say to the wind and the waves?

2. What did the bleeding woman have to do to be healed by Jesus?

3. Jesus told the disciples that, following His ascension and in His mighty name, they would be able to drive out demons, speak in new tongues, and do several other miracles. Name two of these other miracles.

 4. Who said the following? "From now on all generations will call me blessed, for the Mighty One has done great things for me."

5. What was Jesus doing when He was transfigured on the mountain?

 6. What two men from the Old Testament appeared with Jesus at the Transfiguration?

 7. What three disciples were present at the Transfiguration?

 8. Whom did Jesus say He had seen "fall like lightning from heaven"?

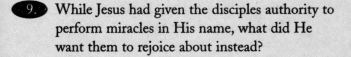 9. While Jesus had given the disciples authority to perform miracles in His name, what did He want them to rejoice about instead?

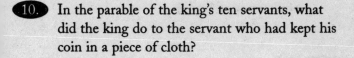 10. In the parable of the king's ten servants, what did the king do to the servant who had kept his coin in a piece of cloth?

How many times did Jesus clear the temple courts of men selling goods and exchanging money?

 When the Jews requested a miraculous sign from Jesus, proving that He had the right to clear the temple the first time, what was Jesus' response?

 In the answer to the previous question, of what temple was Jesus speaking?

 Paul writes to the church in Ephesus, "Be strong in the Lord and in his _____ _____." What two words are missing?

 According to Paul, why should we put on "the full armor of God"?

16. What did the breastplate of the armor of God represent?

17. What two *S* words complete this phrase: "Take the helmet of _____ and the sword of the _____"?

18. Who said the following: "After me will come one more powerful than I, the thongs of whose sandals I am not worthy to stoop down and untie"?

19. Fill in the blank. To the Sadducees who had asked Jesus what marriage would be like in heaven, Jesus told them they were in error because they knew neither the Scriptures nor the _____ of God.

20. Complete this sentence. Instead of taking away Paul's "thorn in my flesh," Jesus said, "My grace is sufficient for you, for my power is made perfect in _____."

Answer Key/Round 7: Mighty God

1. "Quiet! Be still!" (Mark 4:39)
2. Touch His clothes (Mark 5:28–29)
3. Pick up snakes with their hands; drink deadly poison without becoming ill; place hands on sick people and make them well (Mark 16:18)
4. Mary, Jesus' earthly mother (Luke 1:48–49)
5. He was praying (Luke 9:29)
6. Moses and Elijah (Luke 9:30)
7. Peter, John, and James (Luke 9:28)
8. Satan (Luke 10:18)
9. That their names were written in heaven (Luke 10:20)
10. He took the coin (mina) and gave it to the servant who had earned ten minas (Luke 19:24)
11. Two times (John 2:13ff. and Matthew 21:12ff.)
12. "Destroy this temple, and I will raise it again in three days" (John 2:19)
13. His body (John 2:21)
14. "Mighty power" (Ephesians 6:10)
15. So we can take a stand against the devil's schemes (Ephesians 6:11)
16. Righteousness (Ephesians 6:14)
17. Salvation; Spirit (Ephesians 6:17)
18. John the Baptist (Mark 1:7)
19. Power (Matthew 22:29)
20. Weakness (2 Corinthians 12:9)

Your score: _____
(out of a possible 220 points)
Total number of points from all rounds: _____
Total possible points: 1120

Round 7: Mighty God/Wrap-up

Listen to King Jehoshaphat's wise words about our *Mighty God:* "You rule over all the kingdoms of the nations. Power and might are in your hand, and no one can withstand you" (2 Chronicles 20:6).

Jesus' power was demonstrated over and over by His miracles and His relationship to God the Father. Indeed, His power was not limited to improving the lives of the sick and disabled but to controlling the very forces of nature as well. His might continues to be seen in those who courageously spread His gospel, wearing an imaginary suit of armor that will withstand the forces of evil and the diabolical assaults of the evil one, once banished by our mighty God from heaven.

Do I hear the rattle of chain mail bringing up the rear? Round 8 awaits, and the joust of your life.

Round 8:
Redeemer

You've proved yourself all too human thus far, and that isn't about to change anytime soon. Ready for the intermission in your boffo performance?

Time to meet Jesus as *Redeemer*. When He came to earth, Jesus had a clear purpose: to redeem or rescue humankind from their sins. To do this, He had to pay the ultimate ransom. He had to die on the cross.

Isaiah the prophet writes, " 'The Redeemer will come to Zion, to those in Jacob who repent of their sins,' declares the LORD" (Isaiah 59:20).

Ticket sales may be down, but your Redeemer is waiting in the wings. It's time to play. . .*Jesus Link!*

Round 8:
Redeemer

Each question in Round 8 is worth 12 points.
Total number of points in this round: 240

 1. Job said, "I know that my _____ lives."
Complete this sentence.

 2. Besides Job and Isaiah, what other well-known
figure of the Old Testament praised his
Redeemer?

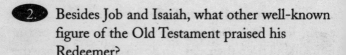 3. To whom did Jesus say, "You don't know what
you are asking. Can you drink the cup I am
going to drink?"

 4. Who were Zebedee's sons?

5. Complete Jesus' sentence: "The Son of Man did not come to be served, but to serve, and to give his life as a _____ for many."

6. After what event did Jesus tell His disciples they would know that their "redemption is drawing near"?

7. What was the other law (besides God's law) Paul saw at work in members of the body of believers?

 8. In his letter to the Romans, Paul says that we "groan inwardly" in eager expectation of what?

 9. On what mountain is the Garden of Gethsemane located?

10. What disciples accompanied Jesus to Gethsemane?

11. What does Golgotha mean?

12. When a soldier pierced Jesus' side with a spear following His death, what flowed out of Jesus?

 13. To whom did Jesus say, "Blessed are those who have not seen and yet have believed"?

14. When Jesus returns to earth for the second time, who will rise to meet Him first?

 15. Paul writes that the "day of the Lord" will come like a "_____ in the night." Complete this sentence.

 16. What *S* word completes this sentence? "For God did not appoint us to suffer wrath but to receive ___ through our Lord Jesus Christ."

 17. As the blood sacrifice for our sins, Jesus the Redeemer is often likened to what Old Testament offering?

18. Peter writes that we were not redeemed by what two perishable things?

19. Why, according to Paul, did Jesus come to redeem "those under law," in other words, the Jews?

20. According to Isaiah, who will be the only ones to walk on God's "highway," the "Way of Holiness" in the new heaven on earth?

ANSWER KEY/ROUND 8: REDEEMER

1. Redeemer (Job 19:25)
2. David (Psalm 19:14)
3. The mother of Zebedee's sons (Matthew 20:20–22)
4. James and John (Matthew 10:2)
5. Ransom (Matthew 20:28)
6. When they would see Jesus coming in a cloud with power and great glory (Luke 21:27–28)
7. The power of sin (Romans 7:23)
8. "Our adoption as sons" and "the redemption of our bodies" (Romans 8:23)
9. Mount of Olives
10. Peter, James, and John
11. The Place of the Skull (Matthew 27:33)
12. Blood and water (John 19:34)
13. Thomas (John 20:29)
14. The dead in Christ (1 Thessalonians 4:16)
15. Thief (1 Thessalonians 5:2)
16. Salvation (1 Thessalonians 5:9)
17. A lamb (see Revelation 5:6–9)
18. Silver and gold (1 Peter 1:18)
19. So they might receive the full rights of sons (Galatians 4:5)
20. The redeemed (Isaiah 35:8–9)

YOUR SCORE: _____
(out of a possible 240 points)
Total number of points from all rounds: _____
Total possible points: 1360

ROUND 8: REDEEMER/WRAP-UP

From the Psalms we read, "No man can redeem the life of another or give to God a ransom for him—the ransom for a life is costly, no payment is ever enough" (Psalm 49:7). Jesus was a man for a time, but He was always a *Redeemer*. Only He had the power to offer His life as a ransom for the sins of the citizens of the world—past, present, and future.

As Paul writes, "In him we have redemption through his blood, the forgiveness of sins, in accordance with the riches of God's grace" (Ephesians 1:7). In Him alone, we have the hope of a future in the new heaven on earth. We have been rescued to spend a perfect eternity with Him.

Feel like making another cameo appearance? Or is it still quiet on the set? Round 9 is next.

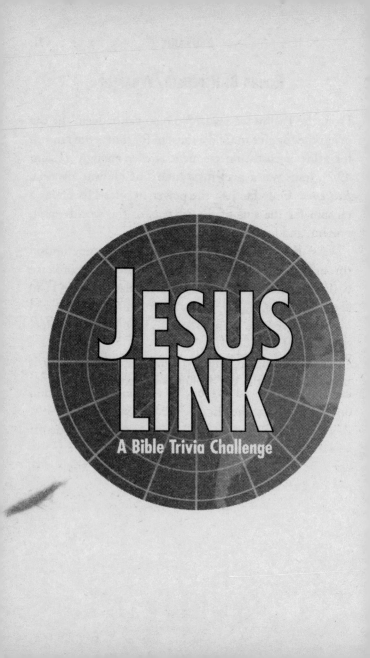

JESUS
LINK

A Bible Trivia Challenge

ROUND 9:
THE ROCK

Now that you've been rescued, in a manner of speaking, it's time to find a safe haven. And what better symbol of safety, security, and trust than a rock? A rock has been the landmark of a new nation, the symbol of a company, and the foundation of buildings.

Now meet *The Rock,* Jesus Christ, a foundation that cannot be destroyed or eroded with time. A foundation on which to base the church, the true body of believers. A foundation to cling to when nothing else seems secure. In a song of praise, David cries out, "The LORD lives! Praise be to my Rock! Exalted be God, the Rock, my Savior!" (2 Samuel 22:47).

Can you carry this tune? It's time to play. . *Jesus Link!*

ROUND 9:
THE ROCK

Each question in Round 9 is worth 13 points.
Total number of points in this round: 260

 1. On what surface did Jesus say a wise man built his house?

 2. On what surface did Jesus say a foolish man built his abode?

 3. What does the name *Peter* mean?

4. While Jesus tells Peter that he will build or lead His church, what does Paul refer to Jesus as, in reference to the church?

 5. Peter writes, "The stone the builders rejected has become the capstone." Who are these builders?

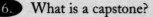 What is a capstone?

7. For whom did Isaiah say that Jesus would be "a stone that causes men to stumble and a rock that makes them fall"?

8. Who said the following of Jesus? "This child is destined to cause the falling and rising of many in Israel."

9. Why did Joseph and Mary bring Jesus to the temple as a baby?

10. During Satan's temptation of Jesus, the evil one told Him to turn a stone into what?

11. Jesus says there will be different reactions to Him, as the Stone. At what time will "he on whom it [this Stone] falls" be crushed?

12. Of what structure did Jesus say, "Not one stone here will be left on another; every one will be thrown down"?

13. On what mount did Jesus preach about the end times and on what same mount did a certain Old Testament minor prophet predict that Jesus would return to that very spot to fight against all nations?

14. Who was the minor prophet mentioned in the previous question?

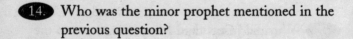

15. In one of King Nebuchadnezzar's dreams, what is the rock that was cut out of the dazzling statue, divinely interpreted by Daniel?

16. To him who overcomes, Jesus said He would give some "hidden manna" and what else?

17. What would be written on the second gift mentioned in the previous question?

18. Paul says we have a building in heaven, an eternal house, not built by human hands. According to him, what is our dwelling here on earth?

19. Complete this sentence from the Book of Hebrews: "For every house is built by someone, but God is the builder of _____."

20. David writes in the Psalms, "He lifted me out of the slimy pit, out of the mud and mire." Where did God then place him?

Answer Key/Round 9: The Rock

1. On rock (Matthew 7:24)
2. On sand (Matthew 7:26)
3. Rock (Matthew 16:18)
4. As the church's cornerstone (Ephesians 2:20)
5. Anyone who refuses to believe in Jesus, the Stone or Rock (1 Peter 2:7)
6. Another word for cornerstone
7. Both houses of Israel (Isaiah 8:14)
8. Simeon, upon seeing Jesus as a baby (Luke 2:34)
9. To consecrate Him to the Lord (Luke 2:23)
10. Bread (Luke 4:3)
11. At the Last Judgment (Matthew 21:44)
12. The temple in Jerusalem, destroyed by the Romans in A.D. 70 (Matthew 24:2)
13. Mount of Olives (Matthew 24:3; Zechariah 14:4)
14. Zechariah
15. God's kingdom that will never be destroyed (Daniel 2:44)
16. A white stone (Revelation 2:17)
17. The believer's new name, given by Jesus (Revelation 2:17)
18. An earthly tent (2 Corinthians 5:1)
19. Everything (Hebrews 3:4)
20. On a Rock (Psalm 40:2)

Your score: _____

(out of a possible 260 points)
Total number of points from all rounds: _____
Total possible points: 1620

ROUND 9: THE ROCK/WRAP-UP

"From the ends of the earth I call to you," writes David. "I call as my heart grows faint; lead me to the rock that is higher than I. For you have been my refuge, a strong tower against the foe" (Psalm 61:2–3).

From the Old Testament to the New, Jesus has been the symbol of strength and everlasting help, so it is fitting that He be called the cornerstone of His church and the architect and builder of a permanent home in heaven. As we await receiving our new name and occupying our perfect home, we can still cling to *The Rock* in times of turmoil, and find rest in Him.

Time to move on—there's plenty more where this came from. Round 10 is another formidable (I use the word literally) challenge for a formidable (I use the word loosely) foe.

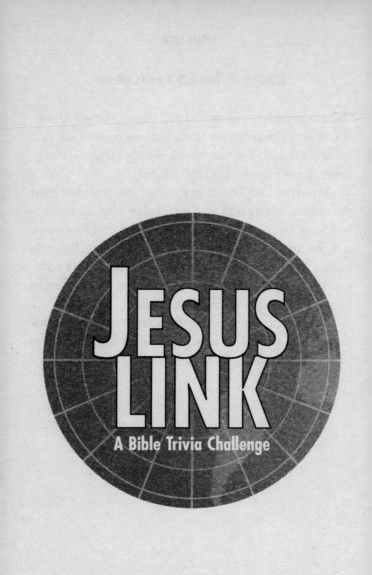

Round 10:
Immanuel

Does it seem like we're going in circles? Or are you suffering from a case of altitude sickness, being on a higher plane than usual?

We've seen Jesus in all His glory as Creator, Father, and Mighty God. We've seen Him as the ultimate caregiver and protector. And now we're back to Bethlehem, to the fulfillment of the prophecy regarding His birth.

As Matthew writes in his Gospel, "All this took place to fulfill what the Lord had said through the prophet: 'The virgin will be with child and will give birth to a son, and they will call him Immanuel'—which means, 'God with us'" (Matthew 1:22–23).

Keep those oxygen canisters handy. It's time to play. . .*Jesus Link!*

ROUND 10:
IMMANUEL

Each question in Round 10 is worth 14 points.
Total number of points in this round: 280

 1. What prophet had the Lord spoken through to reveal the name Immanuel?

 2. To whom did Mary say, "How will this be, since I am a virgin?"

 3. What did Joseph have in mind to do once Mary was found to be "with child"?

4. What relative, who was also pregnant, did Mary visit after receiving her most blessed news?

5. Why did Joseph and Mary travel to Bethlehem in the first place?

6. What widow approached Mary and Joseph in the temple, where they had gone to consecrate the baby Jesus to the Lord?

7. Who was king of Judea at the time of Jesus' birth?

8. Why did Joseph and Mary take Jesus to Jerusalem when He was twelve years old?

9. How did Jesus at age twelve refer to the temple in Jerusalem?

10. When does God Himself first acknowledge Jesus' presence on earth in a verbal declaration from heaven?

Where did Jesus proclaim the following? "The Spirit of the Lord is on me, because he has anointed me to preach good news to the poor. . . to proclaim the year of the Lord's favor."

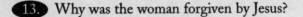 What do we know of the woman who brought an alabaster jar of perfume to the house of a Pharisee where Jesus was dining?

 Why was the woman forgiven by Jesus?

14. Although not denying His earthly family, who did the man Jesus say his mother and brothers were?

15. In answer to Jesus' query, who did Peter say the crowds of people thought He was?

 Immediately afterward, who did Peter say Jesus was?

Which of Jesus' disciples said the following? "But, Lord, why do you intend to show yourself to us and not to the world?"

18. To whom did Jesus say, "You would have no power over me if it were not given to you from above"?

19. What three events happened immediately after Jesus "gave up his spirit"?

20. What did the centurion and other guards say following these cataclysmic events?

ANSWER KEY/ROUND 10: IMMANUEL

1. Isaiah (Isaiah 7:14)
2. The angel Gabriel (Luke 1:34)
3. Divorce her quietly (Matthew 1:19)
4. Elizabeth, pregnant with John the Baptist (Luke 1:39–40)
5. For a census ordered by Caesar Augustus (Luke 2:1–4)
6. Anna, the daughter of Phanuel (Luke 2:36)
7. Herod the Great (Matthew 2:1)
8. To celebrate the Feast of the Passover (Luke 2:41–42)
9. As His Father's house (Luke 2:49)
10. At Jesus' baptism by John the Baptist (Luke 3:22)
11. At the synagogue in Nazareth (Luke 4:16–19)
12. That she had led a sinful life (Luke 7:37)
13. Because she loved much, as demonstrated by her pouring perfume on Jesus' feet (Luke 7:47)
14. Those who hear God's Word and put it into practice (Luke 8:21)
15. John the Baptist, Elijah, or other prophets come back to life (Luke 9:18–19)
16. "The Christ of God" (Luke 9:20)
17. Judas (not Judas Iscariot) (John 14:22)
18. Pontius Pilate (John 19:10–11)
19. (a) The curtain of the temple was torn in two, from top to bottom; (b) there was an earthquake; (c) tombs broke open and many holy people were raised to life and began wandering in Jerusalem (Matthew 27:51–53)
20. "Surely he was the Son of God!" (Matthew 27:54)

YOUR SCORE: _____

(out of a possible 280 points)

Total number of points from all rounds: _____

Total possible points: 1900

ROUND 10: IMMANUEL/WRAP-UP

His birth was predicted hundreds of years before it occurred. Even when He was a baby, there were those in the temple who recognized that God was indeed with us. *Immanuel* had finally arrived. The long-awaited promise to Israel was at last fulfilled.

Still, from Herod the Great to the Pharisees to the crowds in Jerusalem who demanded His crucifixion, there were many who refused to believe the truth that walked among them. Only after His death, and the otherworldly events that followed, were some doubters finally convinced.

The short life of Jesus on earth would nonetheless not be forgotten. Jesus was unlike any other man who had or would be born because He was—Immanuel.

Time to pack your gear and hit the road. Round 11 is next on the itinerary.

JESUS LINK

A Bible Trivia Challenge

Round 11:
Nazarene

From all those Sunday school lessons you're surely familiar with the early years of Jesus' life on earth. Yes, He was born in Bethlehem, but after a few years Joseph moved the family to the little town of Nazareth.

That was Sunday school. . .this *is* the *Jesus Link!* Time to push the envelope (no, you're not still thanking the Academy). Time to delve into the intricacies of God's Word.

From Matthew's Gospel we read, "So he [Joseph] got up, took the child and his mother and went to the land of Israel. . . . Having been warned in a dream, he withdrew to the district of Galilee, and he went and lived in a town called Nazareth. So was fulfilled what was said through the prophets: 'He will be called a Nazarene' " (Matthew 2:21–23).

It's time to play. . *Jesus Link!*

ROUND 11:
NAZARENE

Each question in Round 11 is worth 15 points.
Total number of points in this round: 300

 1. In what town did the Magi visit the child Jesus?

 2. Why did Joseph then move the family to Egypt?

 3. What minor prophet prophesied of Jesus, "Out of Egypt I called my son"?

4. To what event was the prophet Jeremiah referring when he wrote, "A voice is heard in Ramah, weeping and great mourning, Rachel weeping for her children and refusing to be comforted, because they are no more"?

5. Why did Joseph not settle in Bethlehem when the angel told him to return to Israel?

 6. What direction is Nazareth from Bethlehem?

7. What region separated Judea from Galilee?

8. Who said the following to Jesus' disciple Philip: "Nazareth! Can anything good come from there?"

9. Why was Nazareth despised by the Jews?

10. To whom did Jesus say, "Here is a true Israelite, in whom there is nothing false"?

11. Where did the anonymous person live who said, "Isn't this the carpenter? Isn't this Mary's son. . . ?"

12. Why did the people of Nazareth reject Jesus?

13. Where did Jesus say that a prophet is without honor?

14. What miracles was Jesus able to do in Nazareth, if any?

15. What "amazed" Jesus about the people of His hometown?

16. Nazareth is (approximately) ten miles away (in different directions) from what two towns in Galilee where Jesus performed miracles of note?

17. What major body of water is less than twenty miles from Nazareth?

18. What river connects the Sea of Galilee with the Dead Sea?

19. What mount approximately five miles from Nazareth is reputed to be the traditional site of the Transfiguration?

20. Who was Archelaus?

ANSWER KEY/ROUND 11: NAZARENE

1. Bethlehem (Matthew 2:8)
2. Because an angel of the Lord had said that King Herod intended to kill Jesus (Matthew 2:13)
3. Hosea (11:1)
4. The slaughter by King Herod of all baby boys two years and younger in the vicinity of Bethlehem (Matthew 2:16–18)
5. Because Herod's son was on the throne (Matthew 2:22)
6. North, approximately seventy miles
7. Samaria
8. Nathanael, who would become one of the twelve (John 1:46)
9. Because there was a Roman garrison in Nazareth
10. Nathanael (John 1:47)
11. Nazareth (Mark 6:3)
12. Because the people in His hometown saw Him only as a carpenter or local boy and not as a teacher and prophet
13. In his hometown (Mark 6:4)
14. Lay His hands on sick people and heal them (Mark 6:5)
15. Their lack of faith (Mark 6:6)
16. Cana (northwest) and Nain (southeast)
17. The Sea of Galilee
18. The Jordan River
19. Mt. Tabor
20. The son of Herod the Great, who succeeded his father in 4 B.C. and was in charge of Judea, Samaria, and Idumea.

YOUR SCORE: _____

(out of a possible 300 points)
Total number of points from all rounds: _____
Total possible points: 2200

ROUND 11: NAZARENE/WRAP-UP

Clearly, the prophecies of Old Testament major and
minor prophets were designed to keep Jesus safe in the
early years of His life on earth. To Joseph, who was a carpenter and not the most learned of men, these prophecies
were conveyed through an angel of the Lord.

Hence, Jesus moved from Bethlehem to Egypt to
Nazareth before embarking on His preordained ministry.
Even when He returned to Nazareth only to be rebuffed,
His trip had been envisioned hundreds of years earlier by
the prophet Jeremiah (see Jeremiah 12:5–6).

Yes, He would be called a *Nazarene*, but to most
people Jesus encountered during His brief ministry He
would be so much more. Ready to trade in the maps for
some real direction? Round 12 is next.

ROUND 12:
MESSIAH
(THE CHRIST)

We're about to move from the specific to the general—
guaranteed to throw most VBS veterans for a curve.

Time to meet *Messiah*, a name derived from the
Hebrew word *masiah*, which means "to anoint with oil."
Although the word *Messiah* is never used in the Old
Testament, the synonym "Anointed One" *is* employed,
replete with prophecies preparing the world for the
arrival of Jesus.

To the woman at the well, Jesus as Messiah is different from Jesus as Counselor or Creator or Father. She said,
"I know that Messiah (called Christ) is coming. When he
comes, he will explain everything to us" (John 4:25).

Pit stop is over. It's time to play. . .*Jesus Link!*

Round 12:
MESSIAH
(THE CHRIST)

Each question in Round 12 is worth 16 points.
Total number of points in this round: 320

 1. What word is the Greek equivalent of *Messiah*?

 2. What reputed sorcerer offered this early Old Testament prophecy of Messiah? "I see him, but not now; I behold him, but not near. A star will come out of Jacob; a scepter will rise out of Israel."

 3. With what does Psalm 45 say that Jesus has been anointed?

 4. How long does the writer of Psalm 45 say God's throne will last?

5. To those who mourn in Zion, Isaiah writes, the Messiah will bestow on them a crown of _____ instead of ashes, and the oil of ____ instead of mourning.

6. But to those who expected a man of kingly demeanor, Isaiah prophesies, "[there was] nothing in his _____ that we should desire him."

7. What famous resident of the Babylonian captivity was able to prophesy the exact number of years from the decree to rebuild Jerusalem until the Messiah would be crucified?

8. In the previous question, how many "sevens" was the length of time?

9. What minor prophet wrote of the Messiah, "See, your king comes to you, righteous and having salvation, gentle and riding on a donkey, on a colt, the foal of a donkey"?

To what event in the life of Jesus was the prophet referring?

 As Jesus rode the donkey toward Jerusalem, what did the people throw down on the road?

 Answering the rebuke of the Pharisees, what *S* word completes Jesus' sentence? "I tell you, if they [the people] keep quiet, the _____ will cry out."

 When Jesus questioned the Pharisees as to whose son was the Christ, what was their reply?

Complete Jesus' answer to the Pharisees: "If then David calls him '_____,' how can he be his son?"

 With whom and to what city was Jesus walking when He said, "How foolish you are, and how slow of heart to believe all that the prophets have spoken! Did not the Christ have to suffer these things and then enter his glory?"

16. According to the apostle John, everyone who believes that Jesus is the Messiah is born of _____.

17. In answer to what question of Pilate's did Jesus reply, "Is that your own idea, or did others talk to you about me?"

18. When Pilate said to the Jews, "Shall I crucify your king?" what was their answer?

19. The inability of the Jews to recognize Jesus as Messiah had been predicted by Jesus: "If you, even you, had only known on this day what would bring you peace—but now it is hidden from your eyes." On what occasion did Jesus say those words?

20. What Gospel writer traces the genealogy backward from Jesus to Adam?

ANSWER KEY/ROUND 12: MESSIAH (THE CHRIST)

1. Christ
2. Balaam (Numbers 24:17)
3. The "oil of joy" (Psalm 45:7)
4. "For ever and ever" (Psalm 45:6)
5. Beauty; gladness (Isaiah 61:3)
6. "Appearance" (Isaiah 53:2)
7. Daniel (Daniel 9:25–26)
8. 69 "sevens," or 483 years
9. Zechariah (9:9)
10. Jesus' triumphal entry into Jerusalem riding on a donkey (Matthew 21:2–5)
11. Their cloaks (Luke 19:36)
12. "Stones" (Luke 19:40)
13. The son of David (Matthew 22:42)
14. "Lord" (Matthew 22:45)
15. Two believers on the way to Emmaus (Luke 24:25)
16. God (1 John 5:1)
17. "Are you the king of the Jews?" (John 18:33)
18. "We have no king but Caesar" (John 19:15)
19. His triumphal entry into Jerusalem (Luke 19:42)
20. Luke (3:23–37)

YOUR SCORE: _____
(out of a possible 320 points)
Total number of points from all rounds: _____
Total possible points: 2520

ROUND 12: MESSIAH (THE CHRIST)/WRAP-UP

Jesus was anointed by God to serve a kingship that had no beginning and would know no end. It was a kingship well defined by prophecy and borne out by reality. It is a kingship that will only be fully understood when Jesus returns a second time to establish His kingdom on earth.

Yet the idea of a king such as Jesus was unsettling to many and blasphemous to those in the tight-knit religious community. How could one so humble and unattractive possibly be God's Anointed One?

The answer is summed up by the woman at the well. Only Jesus, the Anointed One, the *Messiah*, the Christ, can tell us things about ourselves we never knew. Only He has the power to change our lives.

Time to get a grip. Round 13 has never been closer.

JESUS
LINK
A Bible Trivia Challenge

ROUND 13:
THE WORD

You've got that dazed look again, signaling to one and all that your game face is on. And just in time, too. We're about to meet Jesus as *The Word*, the living embodiment of Scripture and the author of the Word of God.

In John's Gospel we read, "In the beginning was the Word, and the Word was with God, and the Word was God" (John 1:1). Not only was Jesus the Creator, but He wrote the words that are the absolute and irrevocable link between humankind and God. As Paul writes to Timothy, "All Scripture is God-breathed" (2 Timothy 3:16)—that is, no words were written except by the divine inspiration of Jesus.

The "eye of the tiger" is certainly not new to you. It's time to play. . *Jesus Link!*

ROUND 13:
THE WORD

Each question in Round 13 is worth 17 points.
Total number of points in this round: 340

 1. "Repent, for the kingdom of heaven is near" are the words Jesus used to signal the beginning of what?

2. In what city was Jesus when He uttered those words?

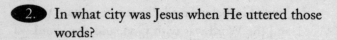 3. To whom was Jesus speaking when He said, "It is written: 'Man does not live on bread alone, but on every word that comes from the mouth of God' "?

 4. How long had Jesus been fasting when He said that?

Jesus was quoting from the Old Testament Book of Deuteronomy. To what episode was the original text referring?

6. While Jesus was in the desert, how many times did Satan tempt Him?

7. When speaking to the Pharisees, who had accused Jesus of being under Satan's power, how did Jesus say one could recognize a tree?

8. What *W* word used twice completes Jesus' sentence: "For by your ___ you will be acquitted, and by your ___ you will be condemned"?

9. To whom must the gospel of Jesus Christ be preached before the end of the world comes, according to Matthew's Gospel?

10. Jesus said, "Heaven and earth will pass away, but my ___ will never pass away." Complete this sentence.

Jesus said, "The Spirit gives life," but what "counts for nothing"?

12. When many followers decided to leave Jesus because of His controversial teachings, how many of the twelve disciples left?

13. Complete Simon Peter's response to Jesus: "Lord, to whom shall we go? You have the ____ of eternal life."

14. Which of the twelve disciples would eventually betray Jesus?

15. Before He was to be betrayed, Jesus prayed for His disciples and for future believers. "Sanctify them by the truth; _____ _____ is truth." Supply the two missing words.

16. In the days of the early church, why did the Grecian Jews complain about the Hebraic Jews?

17. After a compromise was reached, what was to be the role of the original twelve disciples?

18. To what kind of weapon does the writer of Hebrews compare the Word of God?

19. James writes that anyone who listens to the Word and does not do what it says is like a man who does what?

20. What two *L* words complete this verse from Psalms? "Your word is a _____ to my feet and a _____ for my path."

ANSWER KEY/ROUND 13: THE WORD

1. His ministry on earth (Matthew 4:17)
2. Capernaum (Matthew 4:13)
3. Satan (Matthew 4:4)
4. Forty days and forty nights (Matthew 4:2)
5. The Hebrew people wandering in the wilderness for forty years, being fed manna by God
6. Three times (see Matthew 4:1–11)
7. By its fruit (Matthew 12:33)
8. "Words" (Matthew 12:37)
9. The whole world (Matthew 24:14)
10. "Words" (Matthew 24:35)
11. "The flesh" (John 6:63)
12. None (John 6:66–70)
13. "Words" (John 6:68)
14. Judas Iscariot (John 6:71)
15. "Your word" (John 17:17)
16. Because their widows were being overlooked in the daily distribution of food (Acts 6:1)
17. The "ministry of the word of God" (Acts 6:2–4)
18. Double-edged sword (Hebrews 4:12)
19. Looks in a mirror and then forgets what he looks like (James 1:23–24)
20. Lamp; light (Psalm 119:105)

YOUR SCORE: _____
(out of a possible 340 points)
Total number of points from all rounds: _____
Total possible points: 2860

Round 13: The Word/Wrap-up

Like Jesus' eternal kingdom, His words are equally enduring.

Consider the tortured history of the Old Testament and the state of the fledgling church in the New Testament. Then consider the reams of promises and prophecies, all of which have stood (or will stand) the test of time.

No, God's Word will never be extinguished, despite the best efforts of humankind. The words of Jesus endure because they are sharp and penetrating, full of wisdom, truth, hope, and peace. As Paul writes to the Colossians, "Let the word of Christ dwell in you richly as you teach and admonish one another with all wisdom, and as you sing psalms, hymns and spiritual songs with gratitude in your hearts to God" (Colossians 3:16).

Do you still have what it takes to make the *Jesus Link*? Round 14 is the next hurdle.

Round 14:
SAVIOR

We're almost halfway finished, and so far you've managed to "bank" a nice little nest egg. (Or is that lay an egg?)

Time to meet the "one who delivers or sets free," which could only be the definition for Jesus as *Savior*. Jesus is not simply the Savior of the Israelites, as in the Old Testament. Instead, we are about to encounter the One who comes to earth to be the Savior of the entire world. In John's Gospel we read, "Now we have heard for ourselves, and we know that this man really is the Savior of the world" (John 4:42).

If you're feeling a bit scrambled, prepare to poach a few points. It's time to play. . .*Jesus Link!*

ROUND 14:
SAVIOR

Each question in Round 14 is worth 18 points.
Total number of points in this round: 360

 1. What new father made this statement? "He has raised up a horn of salvation for us in the house of his servant David."

 2. What mother-to-be made this statement? "My soul glorifies the Lord and my spirit rejoices in God my Savior."

 3. In the quote from John 4:42 on the preceding page, who is the "we," and to whom are they speaking?

 4. Of whom was Jesus speaking when He said, "Today salvation has come to this house, because this man, too, is a son of Abraham"?

5. What was the occupation of this "son of Abraham"?

6. Complete this sentence: "For God did not send his Son into the world to condemn the world, but to ___ the world through him."

7. On what occasion did Peter offer these remarks? " 'I will pour out my Spirit in those days, and they will prophesy. . .and everyone who calls on the name of the Lord will be saved.' "

8. What tax collector became one of Jesus' twelve disciples?

9. What was the primary occupation of many of Jesus' disciples?

10. What was the "one thing" Jesus told the rich young man that he lacked to inherit eternal life?

To the disciples Jesus said, "It is easier for a
_____ to go through the eye of a needle than for
a rich man to enter the kingdom of God."
Complete this sentence.

 Complete Jesus' sentence: "If anyone would
come after me, he must deny himself and take
up his _____ and follow me."

 Where is our citizenship, according to Paul in
his letter to the Philippians?

 What will our Savior, the Lord Jesus Christ, do
to our bodies once we join Him in heaven?

 In the "Lord's Prayer," Jesus instructs us to pray
to be delivered from what or whom?

 Reading from the Book of Isaiah in the synagogue in Nazareth, Jesus said He had been sent
to proclaim freedom for whom?

17. John writes in Revelation, "To him who loves us and has freed us from our sins by his ____. . . ." Complete this sentence.

18. Salvation will come for the Jewish people, Paul writes to the Romans, before Jesus returns to earth to establish His kingdom. From where will the deliverer come, according to Paul?

19. Isaiah writes, "I, even I, am the LORD, and apart from me there is no _____." Complete this sentence.

20. What is the one requirement Jesus gives for receiving eternal life (salvation)?

ANSWER KEY/ROUND 14: SAVIOR

1. Zechariah, father of John the Baptist (Luke 1:69)
2. Mary (Luke 1:46–47)
3. Many Samaritans are the "we"; they are speaking to the Samaritan woman who encountered Jesus at the well (John 4:39–42)
4. Zacchaeus (Luke 19:9)
5. He was the chief tax collector (Luke 19:2)
6. "Save" (John 3:17)
7. Pentecost (Acts 2:18, 21)
8. Matthew (aka Levi), son of Alphaeus
9. They were fishermen (Peter, James, John, Andrew, and Philip)
10. He must sell everything he has and give to the poor (Mark 10:21)
11. "Camel" (Mark 10:25)
12. "Cross" (Matthew 16:24)
13. In heaven (Philippians 3:20)
14. They will be transformed to appear like Jesus' glorious body (Philippians 3:21)
15. The evil one (Satan) (Matthew 6:13)
16. The prisoners (Luke 4:18)
17. "Blood" (Revelation 1:5)
18. From Zion (Romans 11:26)
19. "Savior" (Isaiah 43:11)
20. To believe in Him (John 3:16)

YOUR SCORE: _____

(out of a possible 360 points)
Total number of points from all rounds: _____
Total possible points: 3220

ROUND 14: SAVIOR/WRAP-UP

Jesus came to save, or deliver, those who were truly lost. This group included people from many walks of life, people with less than stellar pasts, and people who had their priorities mixed up.

That includes everybody, doesn't it? So it almost goes without saying that we all need a *Savior* to obtain eternal life. Only Jesus paid with His blood on the cross to redeem us from all the ugliness of our lives.

To receive this indescribably precious gift of salvation, we must do only one thing: Believe that Jesus is the Son of God. If our belief is sincere, the wonders of the Christian life will follow.

Time to skedaddle. Round 15 is the next obstacle.

JESUS
LINK

A Bible Trivia Challenge

Round 15:
Bread of Life

Don't know when to say when? (Don't let me be the first to tell you.) On you the lean and hungry look is still quite endearing. It's time to find your place at the table.

We are about to meet Jesus as the *Bread of Life*, a title He bestowed on Himself. He is the only sustenance we need; having faith in Him ensures an eternal future. "Jesus declared, 'I am the bread of life. He who comes to me will never go hungry, and he who believes in me will never be thirsty' " (John 6:35).

Are you a glutton for punishment? It's time to play. . . *Jesus Link!*

Round 15:
BREAD OF LIFE

Each question in Round 15 is worth 19 points.
Total number of points in this round: 380

 1. What town that figured significantly in Jesus' earthly life can be translated from the Hebrew as "house of bread"?

2. Complete Jesus' sentence from a parable: "The kingdom of heaven is like ___ that a woman took and mixed into a large amount of flour until it worked all through the dough."

 3. To whom did Jesus say, "Man does not live on bread alone"?

 4. Jesus' response was in answer to what temptation?

5. Instead of fish, Jesus told His disciples they would now catch what?

6. In response to what charge by the Pharisees does Jesus cite the example of David eating consecrated bread?

7. Just prior to feeding the five thousand, where had Jesus been?

 8. Why did the disciples want Jesus to send the crowds away?

9. How many loaves and how many fish were available to feed the five thousand?

10. How many basketfuls of broken pieces were left over, once the crowd was satisfied?

11. To whom was Jesus speaking when He said, "It is not right to take the children's bread and toss it to their dogs"?

12. In the previous question, who are the "children" and who are "their dogs"?

 13. When Jesus fed the four thousand, a separate event from the feeding of the five thousand, where was He?

 14. How long had He been with the people, healing them, without food?

15. How many loaves were distributed this time?

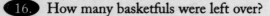

 16. How many basketfuls were left over?

17. In Jesus' parable of the great feast, how many times are invitations issued by the master's servant?

Jesus said, "I am the living bread that came down from heaven. If anyone eats of this bread, he will live forever. This bread is my _____, which I will give for the life of the world." Complete this sentence.

19. What is the name of the feast also called the Passover?

20. What did the bread and wine at Jesus' last supper with His disciples symbolize?

Answer Key/Round 15: Bread of Life

1. Bethlehem
2. "Yeast" (Matthew 13:33)
3. Satan (Luke 4:4)
4. To turn stones into bread (Luke 4:3)
5. Men (Luke 5:10)
6. It was unlawful to harvest food on the Sabbath (Luke 6:1–4)
7. He had withdrawn in a boat to a solitary place (Matthew 14:13)
8. They were in a remote place, far from villages where the people could buy food for themselves (Matthew 14:15)
9. Five loaves and two fish (Matthew 14:17)
10. Twelve basketfuls (Matthew 14:20)
11. A Canaanite woman whose daughter was possessed of demons (Matthew 15:26)
12. The children are the lost sheep of Israel; the dogs were the Gentiles.
13. On a mountainside by the Sea of Galilee (Matthew 15:29)
14. Three days (Matthew 15:32)
15. Seven (Matthew 15:34)
16. Seven (Matthew 15:37)
17. Three times (Luke 14:15–24)
18. "Flesh" (John 6:51)
19. Feast of Unleavened Bread (Luke 22:1)
20. His body and blood, which were to be sacrificed for them (and us) (Luke 22:19–20)

Your score: _____
(out of a possible 380 points)
Total number of points from all rounds: _____
Total possible points: 3600

ROUND 15: BREAD OF LIFE/WRAP-UP

Just as Jesus used parables to convey deep spiritual truths, He used symbolism to depict the power of the Christian faith. Even though He had stated the issue plainly—"I tell you the truth, he who believes has everlasting life" (John 6:47)—there was more to say, in a way that would have particular meaning for His Jewish audience.

While their forebears had feasted on manna in the wilderness, bread that spoiled after a day, Jesus offered them bread that would never spoil and life that would never cease. Likewise, when we partake of communion, eating the matzoh and drinking grape juice, we are saying we believe Jesus, the *Bread of Life*, is the only way to salvation and eternal life.

Time to push back your chair. Round 16 awaits.

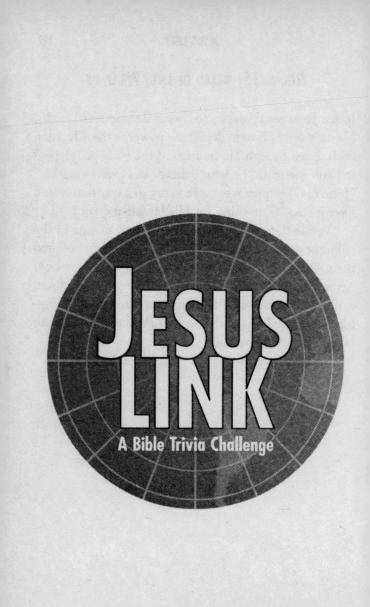

Round 16:
Light of the World

I'd love to think you're a late bloomer, ready to show your true colors in the second half of the game. If you're aching for a dose of photosynthesis, this round is it. We're about to meet Jesus as the *Light of the World!*

John writes in his Gospel, "When Jesus spoke again to the people, he said, 'I am the light of the world. Whoever follows me will never walk in darkness, but will have the light of life'" (8:12). If we walk in His light, our feet will never falter because He is leading us.

It's a beautiful day in the neighborhood. It's time to play. . .*Jesus Link!*

ROUND 16:
LIGHT OF THE WORLD

Each question in Round 16 is worth 20 points.
Total number of points in this round: 400

1. The prophet Isaiah writes, "The people walking in _____ have seen a great light." Complete this sentence.

2. Speaking symbolically, Jesus says that people who light a lamp should do what with it?

3. Jesus calls believers not only "the light of the world" but also "the _____ of the earth."

4. Why, according to Jesus, should we let our light "shine before men"?

5. What body part does Jesus call "the lamp of the body"?

6. Just as we cannot live in light and darkness at the same time, Jesus says we cannot serve two masters. Complete Jesus' sentence: "You cannot serve both God and _____."

7. At what event did Jesus' face shine like the sun and His clothes become as white as the light?

8. In the parable of the four soils, some people, like seeds planted on what kind of soil, are at first glad to hear the Word of God but then are eager only a short time?

9. Seeds sown among thorns yield what kind of people?

10. Speaking of Jesus, the apostle John writes, "In him was life, and that life was the _____ of men." Complete that sentence.

11. John says that to all who receive Jesus, to those who believe in His name, He gives the right to become _____ of God.

12. Why, according to Jesus, have men loved darkness instead of light?

13. To whom was Jesus speaking when He said, "I am the light of the world. Whoever follows me will never walk in darkness, but will have the light of life"?

14. In what area of the temple was Jesus speaking when he was quoted in the previous question?

15. Predicting His death on the cross, Jesus said, "Put your trust in the light while you have it, so that you may become _____ of light." Complete this sentence.

16. Speaking in the synagogue, Paul and Barnabas said, "For this is what the Lord has commanded us: 'I have made you a light for the _____, that you may bring salvation to the ends of the earth.'" Complete this sentence.

17. Paul writes to the Romans, "The night is nearly over; the day is almost here." What does he mean by the day?

18. John writes that if we claim to have fellowship with Jesus but then choose to "walk in the darkness," we are doing what?

19. Peter writes of several "faith qualities" that will keep us from becoming "nearsighted and blind." What quality should first be added to your faith?

20. What quality should be added to "brotherly kindness"?

ANSWER KEY/ROUND 16: LIGHT OF THE WORLD

1. "Darkness" (Isaiah 9:2)
2. Put it on its stand so that it gives light to everyone in the house (Matthew 5:15)
3. "Salt" (Matthew 5:13)
4. So that may see our good deeds and praise our Father in heaven (Matthew 5:16)
5. The eye (Matthew 6:22)
6. "Money" (Matthew 6:24)
7. The Transfiguration (Matthew 17:2)
8. Those planted on rocky soil (Mark 4:16–17)
9. Those that hear the Word but become discouraged by the worries of this life and drift away (Mark 4:18–19)
10. "Light" (John 1:4)
11. Children (John 1:12)
12. Because their deeds were evil (John 3:19)
13. To the Pharisees in the temple (John 8:12–13)
14. Near the place where the offerings were put—in this area candles were burned to symbolize the pillar of fire leading the Israelites through the wilderness (John 8:20)
15. "Sons" (John 12:36)
16. "Gentiles" (Acts 13:47)
17. The time of Jesus' return (Romans 13:12)
18. We are lying and not living by the truth (1 John 1:6)
19. Goodness (2 Peter 1:5, 9)
20. Love (2 Peter 1:7)

YOUR SCORE: _____
(out of a possible 400 points)
Total number of points from all rounds: _____
Total possible points: 4000

Round 16: Light of the World/Wrap-up

When we have heard Jesus' words and believe that He is the Son of God, we no longer want to walk in the darkness of lies and evil deeds but in the light of His truth. This is what it means to walk in the light: living the truth.

But walking in the light implies a sense of responsibility, too. We now are called by Jesus to be witnesses for Him, showing our good deeds for all to see while praising God for His many blessings. Furthermore, when we walk in the light, we become members of the family of God—we become known as children of God!

Feel a growth spurt coming on? Round 17 is next.

Round 17:
Son of Man

You've probably been the recipient of many nicknames (even though you always answered to "Dinner!"). Some were likely foisted upon you because of your appearance or personality, while others may have been due to a family relationship. Undoubtedly, among the telling array, you had a favorite moniker that you encouraged others to use.

Judging simply from the number of times He used it to refer to Himself, Jesus, too, had a favorite name: *Son of Man.* While the name is a testimony to Jesus' servanthood, it has other meanings as well. Mark writes, "For even the Son of Man did not come to be served, but to serve, and to give his life as a ransom for many" (Mark 10:45).

You're on call. It's time to play. . *Jesus Link!*

ROUND 17:
SON OF MAN

Each question in Round 17 is worth 21 points.
Total number of points in this round: 420

1. In what Old Testament book is the name "son of man" introduced? (*Hint:* The writer saw the son of man in a vision.)

2. Who will inherit the earth, according to Jesus in what came to be known as "The Beatitudes"?

3. What creatures did Jesus cite as having homes when "the Son of Man has no place to lay his head"?

4. To whom was Jesus speaking in the previous question?

5. To the man who wanted to say good-bye to his family before following Jesus, Jesus replied, "No one who puts his hand to the _____ and looks back is fit for service in the kingdom of God." Complete this sentence.

 6. What did the erstwhile disciple want to do before receiving this command from Jesus: "Follow me, and let the dead bury their own dead"?

 7. In what city was a paralyzed man lowered through a roof to see Jesus?

 8. When Jesus saw the paralyzed man, what did He say first, much to the consternation of the teachers of the law?

9. Whom did Jesus say "has authority on earth to forgive sins"?

10. Speaking of the end times, Jesus said, "I tell you the truth, you will not finish going through the cities of _____ before the Son of Man comes." Complete this sentence.

11. Condemning public opinion, Jesus said that while the Son of Man came "eating and drinking," people called Him a friend of whom?

12. When the Pharisees asked for a "miraculous sign" from Jesus, Jesus said none would be given— except the sign of what Old Testament prophet?

13. How was this prophet's experience analogous to the Son of Man's future burial?

14. When the Son of Man sits on His glorious throne, Jesus says, who will sit on twelve thrones with Him?

15. Complete Jesus' sentence: "For as lightning that comes from the east is visible even in the west, so will be the coming of the _____ _____ _____"[three words].

16. At what hour do three Gospel writers say the Son of Man will come again?

17. Jesus says of the man who betrayed the Son of Man, "It would be better for him if _____ _____." Complete this sentence (5 words).

18. To the high priest of the Sanhedrin who questioned if Jesus were the Son of God, Jesus said that he would see the Son of Man in the future doing what?

19. Who was this high priest?

20. In the Book of Revelation, whom does the apostle John see among the seven golden lampstands, dressed in a long robe with a golden sash?

Answer Key/Round 17: Son of Man

1. Daniel (Daniel 7:13)
2. The meek (Matthew 5:5)
3. Foxes and birds (Luke 9:58)
4. A teacher of the law (Matthew 8:19–20)
5. "Plow" (Luke 9:62)
6. Bury his father (Matthew 8:21–22)
7. Capernaum (Mark 2:1)
8. "Son, your sins are forgiven" (Mark 2:5)
9. The Son of Man (Mark 2:10)
10. "Israel" (Matthew 10:23)
11. Tax collectors and sinners (Matthew 11:19)
12. Jonah (Matthew 12:39)
13. Jonah spent three days and nights in the belly of a big fish; Jesus would remain buried for the same amount of time (Matthew 12:40)
14. Jesus' twelve disciples (Matthew 19:28)
15. "Son of Man" (Matthew 24:27)
16. At an hour when you do not expect Him (Matthew 24:44; Mark 13:33; Luke 21:34)
17. "He had not been born" (Matthew 26:24)
18. "Sitting at the right hand of the Mighty One and coming on the clouds of heaven" (Matthew 26:64)
19. Caiaphas (Matthew 26:57)
20. The Son of Man (Revelation 1:13)

Your score: _____

(out of a possible 420 points)
Total number of points from all rounds: _____
Total possible points: 4420

ROUND 17: SON OF MAN/WRAP-UP

The name *Son of Man* immediately conjures up images of one serving another human being. Even though Jesus spent countless hours teaching and healing, what was more important to Him than physical healing was the saving of the soul and the forgiveness of sins. Only the Son of Man had the power to forgive human sin.

Yet, Jesus Himself wants you to know another Son of Man, One who one day will rule over all peoples on a glorious throne in a kingdom that will defy all adjectives. Indeed, this most-used name of Jesus implies not only the possibilities of the Christian faith on earth, but also the glories of our future home with our Lord.

Ready to answer to a new name? Round 18 has your number.

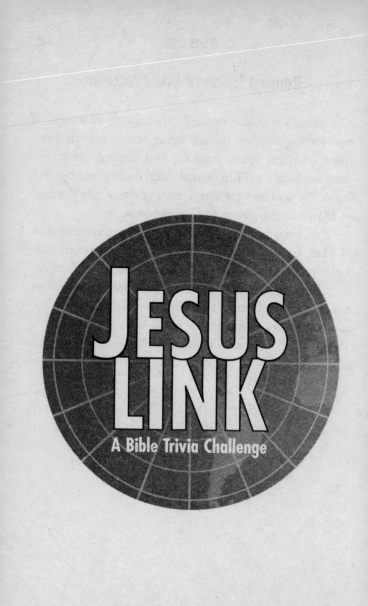

ROUND 18:
RABBI

Time to put our heads on our desks while all the merry sounds of the playground waft through the open windows. Recess ended awhile ago, but far be it from me to deny you the memory of a mountaintop experience.

We're about to meet Jesus as *Rabbi*, the Hebrew name that means "teacher." The consummate teacher, Jesus knew His audience and the best ways to reach them. So commanding was He that even His disciples used this name to describe Him. "Then Nathanael declared, 'Rabbi, you are the Son of God; you are the King of Israel'" (John 1:49).

There is no substitute teacher for Jesus. It's time to play. . *Jesus Link!*

ROUND 18:
RABBI

Each question in Round 18 is worth 22 points.
Total number of points in this round: 440

1. What man did Jesus address as "Israel's teacher"?

2. For the celebration of which feast did Jesus arrive in Jerusalem secretly, instead of publicly as His earthly brothers wished?

3. To the amazement of the Jews in the temple court of Jerusalem, Jesus said His teaching came from whom?

4. When Jesus discovered that His friend Lazarus was sick, He said that the sickness was for God's _____.

5. Who told Jesus that Lazarus was ill?

6. How long was Lazarus in the tomb before Jesus arrived at the site in Bethany?

7. Because of what miracle did the Sanhedrin plot to take Jesus' life?

8. Before what event in His earthly life did Jesus wash His disciples' feet?

9. Complete Jesus' sentence: "Now that I, your Lord and _____, have washed your feet, you also should wash one another's feet."

10. "If anyone loves me," Jesus said, "he will obey my _____." Complete this sentence.

11. When Mary Magdalene heard Jesus say her name following His resurrection, how did she address Him?

12. What did Jesus' disciples ask Him to teach them to do, "just as John [the Baptist] taught his disciples"?

13. While it is a sin to commit adultery, what did Jesus teach about lust?

14. What did Jesus teach about taking oaths or vows?

15. Where did Jesus teach that we should pray?

16. Teaching about worry, why did Jesus say we shouldn't fret about tomorrow?

17. What *P* word describes the stories Jesus told as teaching tools?

18. Why was the mustard seed used by Jesus to illustrate the kingdom of heaven?

What did the pearl merchant do after finding a pearl of great value?

20. Whom did Jesus say is the only one that should be called teacher?

ANSWER KEY/ROUND 18: RABBI

1. Nicodemus (John 3:9–10)
2. Feast of the Tabernacles (John 7:2, 10)
3. From God (John 7:16)
4. Glory (John 11:4)
5. Mary and Martha, Lazarus's sisters (John 11:1, 3)
6. Four days (John 11:17)
7. Raising Lazarus from the dead (John 11:53)
8. On the night before His crucifixion (John 13:1, 5)
9. "Teacher" (John 13:14)
10. "Teaching" (John 14:23)
11. "Rabboni!" (John 20:16)
12. To pray (Luke 11:1)
13. Anyone who looks at a woman lustfully has already committed adultery in his heart (Matthew 5:28)
14. Do not take oaths or vows; your word should be enough (Matthew 5:34–37)
15. In a room with the door closed (Matthew 6:6)
16. Each day has enough troubles (Matthew 6:34)
17. Parables
18. Because it was the smallest of all seeds that grows to become the largest of garden plants (Matthew 13:31–32)
19. He sold everything he had and bought the pearl (Matthew 13:45–46)
20. The Christ (Matthew 23:10)

YOUR SCORE: _____

(out of a possible 440 points)
Total number of points from all rounds: _____
Total possible points: 4860

ROUND 18: RABBI/WRAP-UP

Jesus as *Rabbi* used several techniques to instruct His wide variety of students. To His disciples He used straight talk, to the masses and even His close personal friends He performed miracles that erased any doubt of who He was, and to peoples of all ages and backgrounds He spoke in parables. Never one to patronize, Jesus spoke on the same level as His listeners, as illustrated by His encounter with the learned Nicodemus.

After delving into the Rabbi's teachings, perhaps we, too, can proclaim with the psalmist, "I have more insight than all my teachers, for I meditate on your statutes. I have more understanding than the elders, for I obey your precepts. . . . I have not departed from your laws, for you yourself have taught me" (Psalm 119:99–100, 102).

Time to stop chewing that pencil. Round 19 looms mightily.

ROUND 19:
THE GOOD SHEPHERD

Perhaps you've had these feelings *very* recently: Where is my life going? Why am I here? How come I feel afraid (but not, curiously, of going bald)? Why do I have a craving for green grass?

Strike that last one, but you will have to admit we do share some common ground with the common sheep. No wonder the Bible is full of ovine references, and little surprise that Jesus gave Himself the name the *Good Shepherd:* "I am the good shepherd. The good shepherd lays down his life for the sheep" (John 10:11).

Try not to go astray in this round. It's time to play. . . *Jesus Link!*

ROUND 19:
THE GOOD SHEPHERD

Each question in Round 19 is worth 23 points.
Total number of points in this round: 460

1. What well-known Old Testament figure is speaking in this passage from Genesis? "May the God before whom my fathers Abraham and Isaac walked, the God who has been my shepherd all my life to this day. . .may he bless these boys."

2. Who are "these boys" to whom the speaker from the previous question refers?

3. When Moses asks God to appoint "a man over this community. . .so the LORD's people will not be like sheep without a shepherd," whom does God appoint?

Which Old Testament book contains many chapters written by a former shepherd who became a king?

5. Ezekiel writes, "I will place over them one shepherd, my servant _____, and he will tend them; he will tend them and be their shepherd." Who is this servant literally and figuratively? (2 answers)

6. What Old Testament minor prophet did Herod's chief priests and teachers of the law quote when describing the Messiah as "a ruler who will be the shepherd of my people Israel"?

7. Who were the first human visitors to see the baby Jesus?

8. Who did Jesus describe as wearing sheep's clothing while inside they are "ferocious wolves"?

9. What was Jesus' reaction to the crowds that followed Him, who, in Matthew's words, were like "sheep without a shepherd"?

10. To what animals did Jesus liken His disciples and the unbelievers to whom they would be sent?

11. To whom did Jesus say, "How much more valuable is a man than a sheep!" and why?

12. In Jesus' illustration, what does the man do who loses one sheep out of one hundred?

13. How does the man feel if he finds the missing sheep?

14. When Jesus someday sits on His throne, how will He be like a shepherd? Who will figuratively go on his right and on his left?

15. Jesus quoted a prophecy of Zechariah when He said, " 'I will strike the shepherd, and the sheep of the flock will be scattered.' " Who were the "sheep of the flock" and why did they scatter?

16. Who is the man, Jesus says, who does not enter the sheep pen by the gate but climbs in some other way?

17. Who enters the sheep pen by the gate?

18. Why do the sheep follow the shepherd?

19. How many flocks and how many shepherds are there?

20. According to the apostle Peter, writing in an epistle, what will the "Chief Shepherd" bestow on worthy elders one day?

ANSWER KEY/ROUND 19: THE GOOD SHEPHERD

1. Jacob (Genesis 48:15–16)
2. Ephraim and Manasseh, Joseph's sons (Genesis 48:13)
3. Joshua (Numbers 27:16–18)
4. Psalms
5. "David" (literally) and Messiah (figuratively) (Ezekiel 34:23)
6. Micah (5:2; Matthew 2:6)
7. Shepherds (Luke 2:8ff.)
8. False prophets (Matthew 7:15)
9. He had compassion on them (Matthew 9:36)
10. Sheep among wolves (Matthew 10:16)
11. To the Pharisees, illustrating it is lawful to do good works on the Sabbath (Matthew 12:12)
12. He leaves the ninety-nine other sheep and goes to look for that one (Matthew 18:12)
13. Happier about that one than the ninety-nine others (Matthew 18:13)
14. He will separate people one from another; "sheep" will go on His right; "goats" on His left (Matthew 25:32–33)
15. The "sheep" were Jesus' disciples who scattered after His arrest (Matthew 26:31; Zechariah 13:7)
16. A thief and a robber (John 10:1)
17. The shepherd of the sheep (John 10:2)
18. They know only his voice (John 10:4)
19. One flock and one shepherd (John 10:16)
20. The crown of glory (1 Peter 5:4)

YOUR SCORE: _____

(out of a possible 460 points)
Total number of points from all rounds: _____
Total possible points: 5320

Round 19: The Good Shepherd/Wrap-up

The prophet Isaiah offers a beautiful picture of Jesus as the *Good Shepherd:* "He tends his flock like a shepherd: he gathers the lambs in his arms and carries them close to his heart; he gently leads those that have young" (Isaiah 40:11).

Like the God of the patriarchs leading His people Israel, Jesus leads those who believe in Him—to greener pastures, to safety, and ultimately to eternal life. He cares about each one of us so much that He was willing to lay down His life for us. As believers, we can know that we are His by the sound of His voice, now gently speaking to our hearts. There is only one true voice and there is only one true Shepherd, Jesus Christ.

Still part of the flock? Round 20 will be new terrain.

JESUS
LINK
A Bible Trivia Challenge

Round 20:
The Branch
(and the Vine)

Hard to believe, but you're well on your way to making. . .the *Jesus Link!* And, not to worry, your secret life as a Bible scholar is in no danger of being exposed. We labor on.

Again, we need to step back in time, before Jesus' birth on earth, to move ahead. We have already met Jesus as Root of Jesse (and David)—and now we will meet Him as the *Branch* of that developed and flourishing family tree (we will also see that He is called the *Vine,* or the source of all fruitfulness). The prophet Jeremiah writes, " 'The days are coming,' declares the LORD, 'when I will raise up to David a righteous Branch' " (Jeremiah 23:5).

That day has come. It's time to play. . .*Jesus Link!*

Round 20:
THE BRANCH
(AND THE VINE)

Each question in Round 20 is worth 24 points.
Total number of points in this round: 480

 1. What two *J* words does Jeremiah use to describe what will happen when the righteous Branch does what is right and just: "In those days _____ will be saved and _____ will live in safety."

2. In Zechariah's vision of the future, to whom does the Lord say that He is going to bring His servant, the Branch?

 3. When Jesus said He is the "true vine," who does He say is the gardener?

What branches of the vine does the gardener cut off?

 No branch can bear fruit unless it does what?

6. What happens to the branches that are thrown away?

7. Jesus has chosen us and appointed us to do what?

 How did Jesus say you could recognize a tree?

9. Complete Jesus' sentence: "For out of the overflow of the ____ the mouth speaks."

10. John the Baptist preached a message similar to that of Jesus. Why did he chide the crowds for claiming, "We have Abraham as our father"?

11. Complete John's sentence: "The _____ is already at the root of the trees."

12. Paul writes to the Romans, "If some of the branches have been broken off, and you, though a wild olive shoot, have been grafted in among the others and now share in the nourishing sap. . ." Who are the wild olive shoots?

13. To live a life worthy of the Lord and please Him in every way, writes Paul to the Colossians, we must be "_____ _____ in every good work, _____ in the knowledge of God." Fill in these three words.

14. Name four fruits of Jesus' Spirit (out of nine).

15. When He appointed His disciples, according to Matthew, Jesus gave them the authority to do what?

16. Who were the two sets of brothers among the disciples?

17. Who was named the twelfth disciple after Judas Iscariot died?

18. Which apostle learned in a vision that he could take the gospel to the "unclean" Gentiles?

19. Which man who was not among the original twelve disciples was considered the first martyr of the Christian church?

20. Who does Zechariah say will one day build the temple of the Lord and then sit and rule on His throne? (2 words)

Answer Key/Round 20: The Branch (and the Vine)

1. "Judah"; "Jerusalem" (Jeremiah 33:16)
2. Joshua as the high priest (Zechariah 3:8)
3. His Father (John 15:1)
4. Those that don't bear fruit (John 15:2)
5. Remain in the Vine (John 15:4)
6. They are thrown into the fire and burned (John 15:6)
7. Go and bear fruit that will last (John 15:16)
8. By its fruit (Matthew 12:33)
9. "Heart" (Matthew 12:34)
10. Because each person must ask for forgiveness and lead a new life, not a life based solely on one's heritage (Luke 3:8)
11. "Ax" (Luke 3:9)
12. Gentile Christians (Romans 11:17)
13. "Bearing fruit"; "growing" (Colossians 1:10)
14. Love, joy, peace, patience, kindness, goodness, faithfulness, gentleness, self-control (Galatians 5:22–23)
15. Drive out evil spirits and heal every disease and sickness (Matthew 10:1)
16. Peter and Andrew; James and John (Matthew 10:2)
17. Matthias (Acts 1:26)
18. Peter (Acts 10)
19. Stephen (Acts 6:1–7:60)
20. The Branch (Zechariah 6:12–13)

Your score: _____
(out of a possible 480 points)
Total number of points from all rounds: _____
Total possible points: 5800

Round 20: The Branch (and the Vine)/Wrap-up

With an eye to His "family tree," Jesus is both the Root of Jesse or David and the *Branch* that will sprout from such a root. Spiritually speaking, Jesus is the Branch or the Vine from which all believers are offshoots.

As believers, we can only be grafted from one Vine, and we will only remain fruitful if we stay as part of that Vine. And, oh, how Jesus wants us to be fruitful! That is how we lead pleasing lives: by being fruitful (bringing others to know Jesus as the Christ) and growing in knowledge of Jesus by studying His Word.

Time to pick up the pace. Round 21 draws near.

ROUND 21:
RESURRECTION AND LIFE

You may be a couple rounds short of a perfectly abysmal score, but that hasn't dampened your zest for living on the edge.

Time to meet Jesus as the *Resurrection and Life*, a name He again bestowed upon Himself: "I am the resurrection and the life. He who believes in me will live, even though he dies; and whoever lives and believes in me will never die. Do you believe this?" (John 11:25–26). Indeed, how can we believe Jesus? By accepting Old Testament prophecy and recognizing its fulfillment in the life of Jesus—and by feeling the power of Scripture penetrate into the depths of our beings.

Time to work without a net (but watch for those pesky strands of hair). It's time to play. . .*Jesus Link!*

ROUND 21:
RESURRECTION AND LIFE

Each question in Round 21 is worth 25 points.
Total number of points in this round: 500

1. What Old Testament writer penned the following? "You will not abandon me to the grave, nor will you let your Holy One see decay."

2. What other Old Testament writer, known for his poignant descriptions of the Messiah, wrote, "See, my servant will act wisely; he will be raised and lifted up and highly exalted"?

3. Who was Jesus speaking to when He said, "The Son of Man is going to be betrayed into the hands of men. They will kill him, and on the third day he will be raised to life"?

4. Concerning the previous question, how many times before this admission does Scripture record that Jesus told of His impending death and resurrection?

5. After Jesus' death, who went to Pilate asking for Jesus' body?

6. What two women sat opposite Jesus' tomb after His body had been placed inside?

7. With what request did the chief priests and Pharisees come to Pilate the day after Jesus was buried?

8. When the two women returned to Jesus' grave on the day after the Sabbath, who was sitting on the stone in front of Jesus' tomb and was the first to inform them of Jesus' resurrection?

9. After hearing the women tell of what they had seen at the tomb, according to Luke, which disciple got up and ran there to look for himself?

10. What did the disciple find at the tomb?

11. Following His resurrection, where did Jesus instruct the disciples to begin preaching about repentance and forgiveness of sins in His name?

12. To whom was Jesus speaking when He said, "I am the resurrection and the life"?

 13. Why was it unusual that Jesus would have shared such a deep spiritual testimony with this person, considering the written record of their previous encounter?

14. Complete the apostle John's sentence: "In him [Jesus] was ____, and that ____ was the light of men."

 15. Jesus tells Nicodemus that the Son of Man must be "lifted up" just as what Old Testament figure lifted up the snake?

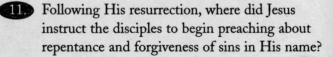

16. What was the first sentence of Jesus' answer in response to this question from a disciple? "Lord, we don't know where you are going, so how can we know the way?"

17. What disciple posed that question?

18. To whom was Jesus speaking when He said, "Do not hold on to me, for I have not yet returned to the Father"?

19. When Jesus teaches about the way to heaven, He describes entering through a gate. What does the gate to heaven look like?

20. Isaiah writes, "But your dead will live; their bodies will rise. You who dwell in the dust, wake up and shout for joy." When will this take place?

ANSWER KEY/ROUND 21: RESURRECTION AND LIFE

1. David (Psalm 16:10)
2. Isaiah (52:13)
3. His disciples (Matthew 17:22–23)
4. Once before (see Matthew 16:24–28)
5. Joseph of Arimathea (Matthew 27:57–58)
6. Mary Magdalene and Mary, mother of James and Joses (Matthew 27:61)
7. To have Jesus' tomb made secure for three days so Jesus' disciples wouldn't steal His body (Matthew 27:63–66)
8. An angel of the Lord (Matthew 28:1–7)
9. Peter (Luke 24:12)
10. Strips of linen laying by themselves (Luke 24:12)
11. In Jerusalem (Luke 24:47)
12. To Martha, Lazarus's sister (John 11:24–25)
13. Martha was usually occupied with household tasks, while her sister Mary was more interested in spiritual matters (see Luke 10:38–42)
14. "Life"; "life" (John 1:4)
15. Moses (John 3:14)
16. "I am the way and the truth and the life" (John 14:6).
17. Thomas (John 14:5)
18. Mary Magdalene (John 20:17–18)
19. Small and narrow and hard to find (Matthew 7:14)
20. When Jesus comes a second time to retrieve His believers, (Isaiah 26:19; 1 Corinthians 15:50–53)

YOUR SCORE: _____
(out of a possible 500 points)
Total number of points from all rounds: _____
Total possible points: 6300

ROUND 21: RESURRECTION AND LIFE/WRAP-UP

Not only did the prophets of old prophesy of Jesus' resurrection, but so did Jesus Himself. Speaking plainly to His disciples, He told them several times that the purpose of His life on earth was to die—as the ransom for the sins of humankind—and then to live again.

When the actual event occurred, the Bible provides many eyewitness accounts. There are, of course, the four Gospels, which together give a complete portrait. But there are individual details as well: Mary Magdalene talking to the angel at the tomb; Peter running as fast as his legs would carry him, only to find scraps of linen remaining.

Still intent on defying reason? Round 22 is next.

JESUS LINK
A Bible Trivia Challenge

ROUND 22:
FRIEND OF SINNERS

Round 22:
Friend of Sinners

Your shortcomings as contestants may be "biggie-sized," but as humans, well, we're all together on the same menu, faults and all. We are all capable 24/7—yup, the drive-through window is always open—of less than stellar thoughts and deeds.

That means we're all sinners, and we sure could use a Friend. Time to meet Jesus, the *Friend of Sinners:* "Behold, . . .a friend of tax collectors and 'sinners',' declares Jesus of Himself, quoting the Pharisees who derided Him (see Matthew 11:19). Indeed, Jesus befriended all kinds of sinners, including, and most especially, those who really needed a Friend.

"Number 22" may be the special you've always wanted to order. It's time to play. . .*Jesus Link!*

ROUND 22:
FRIEND OF SINNERS

Each question in Round 22 is worth 26 points.
Total number of points in this round: 520

1. What did Jesus say we should do to those who persecute us?

2. Which of Jesus' disciples had one of the most hated occupations of the time (and what was it)?

3. What did Jesus ask the man with leprosy to do once He had healed him?

4. What people need a doctor, according to Jesus?

To His disciples, Jesus said, "Freely you have received; freely _____." Complete this sentence.

 What part of a certain handicapped man's body did Jesus heal on the Sabbath?

 Why couldn't Jesus' disciples heal the boy who suffered from seizures and/or demons?

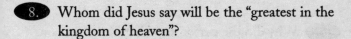 Whom did Jesus say will be the "greatest in the kingdom of heaven"?

 Whom did Jesus say watches over children?

10. When someone wrongs you, what does Jesus say you should do first?

11. To whom did Jesus say, "I tell you the truth, the tax collectors and the prostitutes are entering the kingdom of God ahead of you"?

12. In whose home in Bethany did the woman come to "anoint" Jesus with expensive perfume?

13. After the demon-possessed man answered Jesus, "My name is Legion, for we are many," what did Jesus do to the demons?

14. Who said to Jesus, "Go away from me, Lord; I am a sinful man!"?

15. Why did the person speaking in the previous question say that at that time?

16. What do we know of Mary Magdalene's past from Luke's Gospel?

17. What does Jesus say the angels do when one sinner repents?

18. What did Zacchaeus do so that he could see Jesus?

19. What did Jesus tell the Samaritan woman about her past?

20. To whom did Jesus say, "See, you are well again. Stop sinning or something worse may happen to you"?

ANSWER KEY/ROUND 22: FRIEND OF SINNERS

1. Pray for them (Matthew 5:44)
2. Matthew, who was a tax collector (Matthew 9:9)
3. To tell no one, but to go to offer himself to the priests, as the law dictated (Matthew 8:4)
4. The sick, not the healthy (Matthew 9:12)
5. "Give" (Matthew 10:8)
6. His shriveled hand (Matthew 12:10–13)
7. They didn't have enough faith (Matthew 17:20)
8. Whoever humbles himself like a child (Matthew 18:4)
9. Their angels in heaven (Matthew 18:10)
10. Go and show him his fault, between the two of you (Matthew 18:15)
11. The chief priests and elders (Matthew 21:23, 31)
12. The home of Simon the Leper (Matthew 26:6)
13. Sent them into a herd of pigs (Mark 5:13)
14. Simon Peter (Luke 5:8)
15. He was astonished at the number of fish his partners had caught through Jesus' instructions (Luke 5:9)
16. She was once possessed of seven demons (Luke 8:2)
17. They rejoice in the presence of God (Luke 15:10)
18. He climbed a sycamore-fig tree (Luke 19:3–4)
19. That she had had five husbands and was now living with a man who was not her husband (John 4:18)
20. The invalid man by the pool at Bethesda, whom Jesus had healed (John 5:5, 14)

YOUR SCORE: _____

(out of a possible 520 points)
Total number of points from all rounds: _____
Total possible points: 6820

Round 22: Friend of Sinners/Wrap-up

Jesus came to earth not to "heal" those who were well but those who were struggling with the ill effects of their sin. Rather than distance Himself from those most commonly labeled sinners, Jesus embraced them, even enlisting a tax collector as one of His twelve disciples and a woman who was once possessed of seven demons as one of His inner circle of followers.

The stories of His amazing healing power are peppered throughout the Gospels. But just as frequently we read of Jesus' encounters with the chief priests and Pharisees, men who dared to hold themselves above the common people and dared to question Jesus' motives. Jesus, who claimed His power from God, had the effrontery to be a *Friend of Sinners!* Yes, He alone is worthy of our praise.

We're moving at warp speed now. Round 23 is fast before us.

JESUS
LINK

A Bible Trivia Challenge

ROUND 23:
KING OF KINGS

You seem to be running the gamut (from A to B, or undistinguished to mediocre), so we'll do the same in this round.

It's no small step to go from Friend of Sinners to *King of Kings*, but one shouldn't make the mistake of thinking of Jesus as simply a wise and saintly man who once walked the earth. Indeed, John tells us in the Book of Revelation, "Out of his [Jesus'] mouth comes a sharp sword with which to strike down the nations. 'He will rule them with an iron scepter'. . . . On his robe and on his thigh he has this name written: KING OF KINGS AND LORD OF LORDS" (Revelation 19:15–16).

Ready for a battle royal? It's time to play. . *Jesus Link!*

Round 23:
King of Kings

Each question in Round 23 is worth 27 points.
Total number of points in this round: 540

1. In the Book of Daniel, what king was speaking when he said of the Most High God, "His kingdom is an eternal kingdom; his dominion endures from generation to generation"?

2. Following the advice of the prophet Isaiah, what king prayed the following amid threat of war with Assyria? "O LORD Almighty, God of Israel, enthroned between the cherubim, you alone are God over all the kingdoms of the earth."

3. Who began preaching in the desert of Judea, saying, "Repent, for the kingdom of heaven is near"?

4. Instead of saying, "What shall we eat?" or "What shall we wear?" Jesus says we should seek what first?

5. Complete Jesus' sentence: "For the Son of Man is going to come in his Father's _____ with his angels, and then he will reward each person according to what he has done."

6. After the Transfiguration, Jesus told His disciples not to tell anyone what they had seen until what happened?

7. Jesus said that with God, all things are _____. Complete this sentence.

8. What Jesus said in the previous question was in answer to what question posed by His disciples?

9. When Jesus comes a second time, where will He appear, and on what?

10. At His second coming, whom will Jesus send to gather His believers from the four winds, and from one end of the heavens to the other?

11. When Jesus leaves His disciples to return to heaven following the Resurrection, He tells them He is with them always, to the very end of what?

12. While Jesus spoke in parables to the crowds, to the disciples He said, "The _____ of the kingdom of God has been given to you." Complete this sentence.

13. To whom is the angel Gabriel speaking when he says, "The Lord God will give him the throne of his father David, and he will reign over the house of Jacob forever; his kingdom will never end"?

 14. Of Joseph of Arimathea, who asked to bury Jesus' body, Luke writes, "He was _____ for the kingdom of God." Complete this sentence.

Walking with the two travelers to Emmaus, Jesus says He first had to do what to be able to "enter his glory"?

 What notice did Pilate have prepared and fastened to Jesus' cross?

17. In what languages was the sign written?

18. When asked by the chief priests to amend the wording of the notice, what was Pilate's answer?

19. Writing to Timothy, Paul calls Jesus the "King of kings and Lord of lords, . . .who lives in _____ light, whom no one has seen or can see." Complete Paul's statement.

20. In the Book of Revelation, after what angel sounds his trumpet are loud voices from heaven heard proclaiming, "The kingdom of the world has become the kingdom of our Lord and of his Christ, and he will reign for ever and ever"?

Answer Key/Round 23: King of Kings

1. Nebuchadnezzar (Daniel 4:3)
2. Hezekiah (Isaiah 37:15–16)
3. John the Baptist (Matthew 3:1–2)
4. His kingdom and His righteousness (Matthew 6:33)
5. "Glory" (Matthew 16:27)
6. The Son of Man had been raised from the dead (Matthew 17:9)
7. Possible (Matthew 19:26)
8. "Who then can be saved?" (Matthew 19:25)
9. In the sky on clouds (Matthew 24:30)
10. His angels (Matthew 24:31)
11. The age (Matthew 28:20)
12. "Secret" (Mark 4:11)
13. Mary, earthly mother of Jesus (Luke 1:30, 32, 33)
14. "Waiting" (Luke 23:51)
15. The Christ first had to suffer crucifixion and then be resurrected (Luke 24:26)
16. "JESUS OF NAZARETH, THE KING OF THE JEWS" (John 19:19)
17. Aramaic, Latin, and Greek (John 19:20)
18. "What I have written, I have written" (John 19:22)
19. "Unapproachable" (1 Timothy 6:16)
20. The seventh angel (Revelation 11:15)

Your score: _____

(out of a possible 540 points)
Total number of points from all rounds: _____
Total possible points: 7360

Round 23: King of Kings/Wrap-up

Signs of the glory of Jesus were present during His ministry on earth but were revealed primarily to His disciples. Only Jesus' disciples were present at His transfiguration, and only they were privy to His most revealing teachings. Through the Gospels, we, too, can know Jesus as His disciples and await His second coming. In the meantime, we can be assured that He is with us, even until the end of this age.

The notice Pontius Pilate had attached to Jesus' cross tells only part of the story. Yes, Jesus is the King of the Jews, but He is also the *King of Kings*, One who sits now on His glorious throne in unapproachable light, awaiting our presence with Him.

Time to mosey on. Round 24 inches closer.

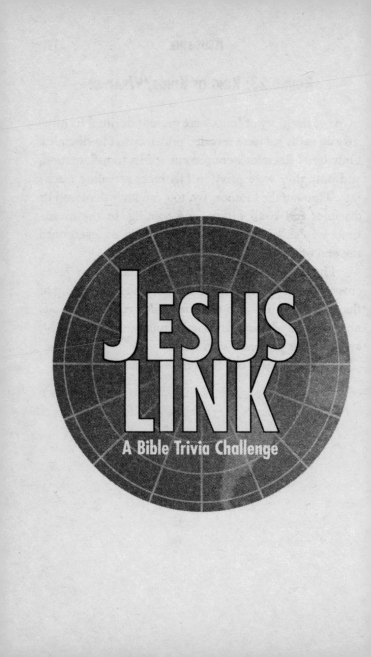

Round 24:
Lord

There are some things you just take for granted. (Once you move away from the breakfast table, life starts to become dicey.)

When you consider the name *Lord* for Jesus, you may feel the same way. He has always been called by that name. . .or has He? Actually, historically speaking, the name Lord (referring to Jesus) was used most frequently after Jesus was resurrected and ascended into heaven, affirming His exalted status and His oneness with His Father. Paul confirms this: "That if you confess with your mouth, 'Jesus is Lord,' and believe in your heart that God raised him from the dead, you will be saved" (Romans 10:9).

Change is good (time for a respectable score!). It's time to play. . .*Jesus Link!*

ROUND 24:
LORD

Each question in Round 24 is worth 28 points.
Total number of points for this round: 560

 1. Complete Jesus' sentence, supplying the same word twice. "Not everyone who says to me, '_____, _____,' will enter the kingdom of heaven, but only he who does the will of my Father who is in heaven."

2. Speaking to the Pharisees, what did Jesus say that David of the Old Testament called the Christ?

3. Speaking to a crowd, Jesus said that all things have been committed to Him by whom?

4. Quoting the Old Testament—"I desire mercy, not sacrifice"—Jesus proclaimed to the Pharisees that He was Lord of the _____.

5. At what occasion was Jesus speaking when He said, "I will not drink of this fruit of the vine. . .until that day when I drink it anew with you in my Father's kingdom"?

6. When Jesus entered Jerusalem riding on a donkey, people shouted, "Blessed is he who comes in the name of the Lord!" They also used what one Hebrew word that means "save"?

7. While speaking to one of the teachers of the law, what did Jesus say was the greatest commandment?

8. Where has the Lord Jesus been since the Ascension, according to Mark's Gospel?

Whose ministry was Isaiah prophesying about when he wrote, "Prepare the way for the LORD, make straight in the wilderness a highway for our God"?

 Following Jesus' resurrection, to what disciple did the other ten say, "We have seen the Lord!"

 Complete Peter's sentence while he was speaking to the crowd at Pentecost: "God has made this Jesus, whom you crucified, both Lord and _____."

 What *I* word describes what Jesus is doing for us at the right hand of God, according to Paul's letter to the Romans?

 Complete Paul's sentence: "So, whether we live or die, we belong to the _____."

14. Paul, writing to the church at Corinth, says that no one can say "Jesus is Lord" except by the power of what?

Paul goes on to say that there is one Lord but there are many kinds of what?

16. Paul describes himself more than once as a ____ for the Lord. Complete this phrase.

17. What name did God give His Son that "is above every name," according to Paul?

18. When Paul writes that Jesus is "head of the body," what body is that?

19. In his letter to the Colossians, Paul writes that in Christ "the fullness of the ____ lives in bodily form." Complete Paul's sentence.

20. Not only is Jesus superior to the angels, says the writer of Hebrews, but "the ____ he has inherited is superior to theirs." Complete this sentence.

ANSWER KEY/ROUND 24: LORD

1. "Lord, Lord" (Matthew 7:21)
2. Lord (Matthew 22:43–45)
3. The Father (Matthew 11:27)
4. Sabbath (Matthew 12:8)
5. The Last Supper (Matthew 26:29)
6. "Hosanna!" (Mark 11:9)
7. " 'Love the Lord your God with all your heart and with all your soul and with all your mind and with all your strength' " (Mark 12:30)
8. In heaven, sitting at the right hand of God (Mark 16:19)
9. John the Baptist's ministry (Isaiah 40:3–5)
10. Thomas (John 20:24–25)
11. "Christ" (Acts 2:36)
12. Interceding (Romans 8:34)
13. "Lord" (Romans 14:8)
14. The Holy Spirit (1 Corinthians 12:3)
15. Gifts or service (1 Corinthians 12:4–5)
16. Prisoner (Ephesians 4:1)
17. Jesus (Philippians 2:9–10)
18. The church (Colossians 1:18)
19. "Deity" (Colossians 2:9)
20. "Name" (Hebrews 1:4)

YOUR SCORE: _____

(out of a possible 560 points)
Total number of points from all rounds: _____
Total possible points: 7920

ROUND 24: LORD/WRAP-UP

While Jesus rode into Jerusalem to the loud praises of the people, who cried "Hosanna!" and blessed Him in the name of the Lord, He would be acknowledged as *Lord* primarily after His ascension into heaven. Since the day of His ascension, Jesus has been seated at the right hand of God the Father, interceding on our behalf.

Jesus is Lord to us when we believe in Him and His Holy Spirit begins to live inside us. Then we can truly use our talents, our God-given gifts, for Him. Only then can we say with Paul that we are privileged to be prisoners for the Lord, privileged to call Him a name superior to even those of the angels.

Round 25 is approaching, and we struggle to get there.

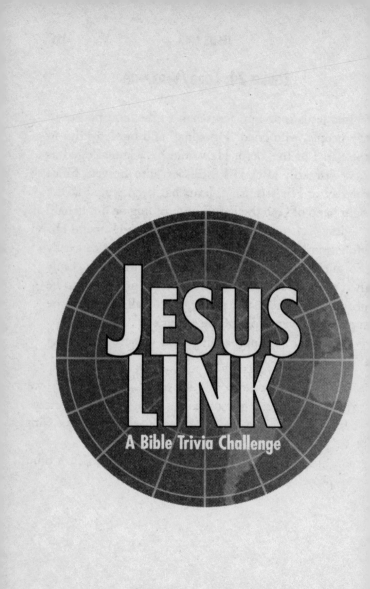

ROUND 25:
HIGH PRIEST

In rounds past, we've pushed the envelope a few times. We've insisted that change is good. (Maybe it's time now to tell you that beige really isn't your color.)

Time to widen the dimensions of your thinking a bit more. Time to meet Jesus as *High Priest*, a title He assumed once He had lived among us, paid the penalty for our sin, and ascended into heaven. "Therefore, since we have a great high priest who has gone through the heavens, Jesus the Son of God, let us hold firmly to the faith we profess" (Hebrews 4:14).

The name itself is reason to feel reassured. It's time to play. . *Jesus Link!*

Round 25:
High Priest

Each question in Round 25 is worth 29 points.
Total number of points in this round: 580

1. The writer of the Book of Hebrews says that as a result of Jesus' death, He has freed those whose lives were held in slavery by their fear of death. Complete this sentence, remembering the source: "For surely it is not angels he [Jesus] helps, but _____ descendants."

2. The same writer goes on to say that in order for Jesus to become a merciful and faithful high priest, He had to do what first?

3. Jesus as high priest is "worthy of greater honor than _____," says the writer of Hebrews, "just as the builder of a house has greater honor than the house itself."

4. To whom did God dictate the first four books of the Bible (and most of the fifth), including the Law?

5. Who was the first high priest of the Old Testament Hebrews?

6. The first high priest came from what tribe?

7. From which of the original twelve tribes was Jesus descended, according to His genealogy?

8. On the Day of Atonement, according to Hebrew law, where was the high priest to offer sacrifices for the sins of the people?

9. Besides the laws for the use of certain animals as sacrifices, what general rule applied to all animals offered to God by the high priest?

10. Though not from the tribe of Levi, the writer of Hebrews says that Jesus has become a high priest forever, in the order of whom?

11. In what book of the Bible is this name first mentioned?

12. What was his title, and what Old Testament patriarch whom he blessed gave him a tenth of his wartime plunder?

13. What were two other titles bestowed on this "priest of God Most High" by the writer of the Book of Hebrews? (*Hint:* Both begin with the words "king of.")

14. What three characteristics does this Old Testament priest share with Jesus, again according to the writer of Hebrews?

15. What other Old Testament king wrote of the Messiah, " 'You are a priest forever, in the order of Melchizedek' "?

16. Unlike the priests of the Old Testament, Jesus does not need to offer sacrifices day after day because "He sacrificed for their sins once for all when he offered _____." Complete this sentence from Hebrews.

17. In what year did animal sacrifices end in the temple in Jerusalem?

18. Paul writes to Timothy, "For there is one God and one _____ between God and men, the man Christ Jesus." Complete this sentence.

19. What was known as the "old covenant" or the "first covenant"?

20. The old covenant was written down, first on stone and then on papyrus. How is the new covenant, one based on grace because of Jesus' sacrificial death, preserved, according to the writer of Hebrews?

ANSWER KEY/ROUND 25: HIGH PRIEST

1. "Abraham's" (Hebrews 2:16)
2. Be made like His brothers (Hebrews 2:17)
3. "Moses" (Hebrews 3:3)
4. Moses
5. Aaron (see Leviticus 16)
6. Levi (Hebrews 7:5)
7. Judah (Hebrews 7:14)
8. The Most Holy Place (see Leviticus 16)
9. They had to be without defect (Leviticus 22:19)
10. Melchizedek (Hebrews 6:20)
11. Genesis (14:18)
12. King of Salem; Abraham (Genesis 14:18–20)
13. King of righteousness and king of peace (Hebrews 7:2)
14. (a) Without father or mother; (b) without genealogy; (c) without beginning of days or end of life (Hebrews 7:3)
15. David (Psalm 110:4)
16. "Himself " (Hebrews 7:27)
17. A.D. 70, with the destruction of the temple in Jerusalem
18. "Mediator" (1 Timothy 2:5)
19. The old covenant was the establishment of the law between Israel and God.
20. In believers' minds and hearts (Hebrews 8:10)

YOUR SCORE: _____
(out of a possible 580 points)
Total number of points from all rounds: _____
Total possible points: 8500

ROUND 25: HIGH PRIEST/WRAP-UP

Like the first high priest appointed by God, Jesus has also been called to serve that esteemed role. But unlike Aaron, a Levite who was required to go through an elaborate procedure to offer animal sacrifices to God, Jesus, a member of the tribe of Judah, had only to offer one sacrifice: Himself.

Jesus is likened more than one time in the Bible to the rather mysterious priest Melchizedek, who carried the title king of Salem but was also known as the king of righteousness and king of peace. Melchizedek, like Jesus, had no known parentage and was, speaking in the syntax of the Bible, without beginning or end of days.

Now as our *High Priest* in heaven, Jesus serves as the mediator between God and His people. There is no need for sacrifice—under the new covenant, we are indeed saved by grace.

Round 26 is next.

JESUS
LINK
A Bible Trivia Challenge

Round 26:
BRIDEGROOM

While you may have a fleeting memory of whatever great works of literature you devoured in high school, your collection of CliffsNotes would likely fill in the blanks.

Remember those pertinent (read: dog-eared) sections on symbolism? Your encyclopedic knowledge of literary devices is about to be tested. Time to meet Jesus as *Bridegroom,* a name He used symbolically for Himself when speaking in parables. "How can the guests of the bridegroom mourn while he is with them? The time will come when the bridegroom will be taken from them; then they will fast" (Matthew 9:15).

No need for neither niceties nor nonsense (alliteration, remember?). It's time to play. . .*Jesus Link!*

Round 26:
Bridegroom

Each question in Round 26 is worth 30 points.
Total number of points in this round: 600

1. Isaiah writes, "As a bridegroom rejoices over his bride, so will your _____ rejoice over you." Complete this sentence.

2. When Jesus answered, "How can the guests of the bridegroom mourn while he is with them," He was responding to what query from John the Baptist's disciples?

3. What symbol did Jesus use to illustrate His new message, the gospel, to John's disciples?

4. On what occasion did Jesus perform His first miracle?

5. When Mary told Jesus that the wine was gone, what was Jesus' response?

6. What did Jesus tell the servants in Cana to do with the six stone water jars?

7. To whom did the master of the banquet in Cana remark, "Everyone brings out the choice wine first. . .but you have saved the best till now"?

8. When the disciples realized that Jesus had performed a miracle, what was their reaction, according to John's Gospel?

9. Continuing the wedding analogy, to whom does John the Baptist compare himself, in awaiting the arrival of Jesus Christ?

10. When is this "member" of the wedding party "full of joy," according to John the Baptist?

11. Complete John the Baptist's sentence: "That joy is mine, and it is now _____. He must become greater; I must become less."

12. In Jesus' parable of the ten virgins who took their lamps and went out to meet the bridegroom, into what two categories does Jesus separate the virgins, and how many were in each category?

13. What did the more frivolous virgins forget to bring with them?

14. When the bridegroom arrived, where were those virgins?

15. What was the bridegroom's reply when five of the virgins begged entrance to the wedding?

16. What is the "moral" of the parable of the ten virgins?

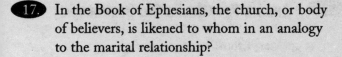 In the Book of Ephesians, the church, or body of believers, is likened to whom in an analogy to the marital relationship?

18. Jesus offered Himself as a sacrifice for the church, to make the church _____—what *H* word is missing?

19. In the Book of Revelation, an angel tells the apostle John to write, " 'Blessed are those who are invited to the wedding supper of the _____!' " Complete this sentence.

20. When John sees the new Jerusalem coming down out of heaven, he compares the city to what?

ANSWER KEY/ROUND 26: BRIDEGROOM

1. God (Isaiah 62:5)
2. "How is it that we and the Pharisees fast, but your disciples do not fast?" (Matthew 9:14–15)
3. New wine (being poured into new wineskins) (Matthew 9:17)
4. A wedding in Cana (John 2)
5. "My time has not yet come" (John 2:4)
6. Fill them with water (John 2:7)
7. The bridegroom (John 2:9–10)
8. They put their faith in Jesus (John 2:11)
9. The friend who attends the bridegroom (John 3:29)
10. When he hears the bridegroom's voice (John 3:29)
11. "Complete" (John 3:29–30)
12. Five virgins were foolish; five were wise (Matthew 25:2)
13. Oil for their lamps (Matthew 25:3)
14. Buying oil for their lamps (Matthew 25:10)
15. "I tell you the truth, I don't know you" (Matthew 25:12)
16. To be ready for Jesus' return, for we do not know when He will come (Matthew 25:13)
17. The bride or wife (Ephesians 5:23–24)
18. Holy (Ephesians 5:26)
19. "Lamb" (Revelation 19:9)
20. A bride beautifully dressed for her husband (Revelation 21:2)

YOUR SCORE: _____

(out of a possible 600 points)
Total number of points from all rounds: _____
Total possible points: 9100

ROUND 26: BRIDEGROOM/WRAP-UP

Jesus came to earth with a new message that was dramatically different from anything anyone had ever heard. To be saved, one needed to believe in Him. Period. Even John the Baptist's followers, who were still consumed with the ramifications of the Old Testament law, were at a loss to understand the gospel completely.

Appropriately, Jesus performed His first miracle at a wedding in Cana, in Galilee. While He was not the actual bridegroom at the ceremony, He had saved the best (wine) for last—indeed, He is our best and only hope for salvation. As He began His ministry and preached in parables, He instructed the crowds to believe now but also to be ready for His second coming at a time that would be hidden from them.

Like the wise virgins, we should have plenty of oil for our lamps when the *Bridegroom* arrives. Like the wise virgins, we should be ready and watchful.

Round 27 is the next test.

ROUND 27:
LAMB OF GOD

Our voyage together is nearing an end, and it's apparent you still haven't found your sea legs. Or maybe the strain on the brain is causing a touch of *mal de mer*?

We're about to encounter a name of Jesus that's probably as familiar to you as terra firma. In the tradition of the Passover sacrifice, Jesus was sent to earth to be the lamb without defect, the *Lamb of God*. Listen to the testimony of John the Baptist as he saw Jesus approaching him: "Look, the Lamb of God, who takes away the sin of the world!" (John 1:29).

Don't "jetsam" with the flotsam just yet. It's time to play. . .*Jesus Link!*

ROUND 27:
LAMB OF GOD

Each question in Round 27 is worth 31 points.
Total number of points in this round: 620

1. What Old Testament patriarch was asked by God to sacrifice his only son?

2. When the son inquired of his father (the patriarch) where they would get the lamb for the burnt offering, what was the patriarch's answer?

3. After the Israelites had slaughtered the Passover lambs, according to Moses' instructions, what were they to do with the lambs' blood?

4. Who died at midnight in Egypt on the night of the first Passover?

5. What was the Passover ceremony to mean to the Israelites, according to God?

 6. What Old Testament prophet described Jesus in this way: "He was oppressed and afflicted, yet he did not open his mouth; he was led like a lamb to the slaughter, and as a sheep before her shearers is silent, so he did not open his mouth"?

7. When the prophet says that Jesus did not open His mouth, what event is he prophesying?

8. In the Book of Acts, who was reading this same portion of Old Testament Scripture when he was approached by the apostle Philip?

9. How many people did Jesus appoint to go, two by two, ahead of Him to various towns to prepare the way for Jesus Himself?

10. To these messengers, Jesus said, "Go! I am sending you out like lambs among _____." Complete Jesus' sentence.

11. In preparation for His final Passover, Jesus instructed His disciples to enter Jerusalem and meet a man carrying what?

12. After following this man, what were the disciples to ask the owner of the house they entered?

13. How does Jesus describe the room where they would eat the Passover?

14. How many times is wine served in Luke's Gospel account of Jesus' last Passover with His disciples?

15. What do the bread and wine symbolize at Jesus' last Passover?

16. Following Jesus' resurrection, what is Jesus' reply when Peter declares the first time that he loves Jesus?

17. When Peter declares for the second time that he loves Jesus, what is Jesus' reply?

18. Writing to the church at Corinth, Paul says, "For Christ, our Passover lamb, has been sacrificed." To keep the feast, or the festival, Paul says we should discard the "old yeast" for bread without yeast, the bread of _____ and _____. Supply these missing words.

19. The great multitude that John sees in the Book of Revelation is dressed in white robes that have been washed in what?

20. In the new Jerusalem, only those whose names are written where will be allowed to enter?

ANSWER KEY/ROUND 27: LAMB OF GOD

1. Abraham (Genesis 22:2)
2. God would provide the lamb (Genesis 22:8)
3. Put some blood on the top and sides of the doorframes of their houses (Exodus 12:22)
4. The firstborn sons of Egypt (Exodus 12:29)
5. God's deliverance of the Hebrews from Egypt (Exodus 12:25–28)
6. Isaiah (53:7)
7. Jesus' questioning by the chief priests and the Sanhedrin (see Mark 14:61)
8. The Ethiopian eunuch (Acts 8:27, 32)
9. 72 (Luke 10:1)
10. "Wolves" (Luke 10:3)
11. A jar of water (Luke 22:10)
12. " 'The Teacher asks: Where is the guest room, where I may eat the Passover with my disciples?' " (Luke 22:11)
13. As a large upper room (Luke 22:12)
14. Two times (Luke 22:17, 20)
15. His body and blood (Luke 22:19–20)
16. "Feed my lambs" (John 21:15)
17. "Take care of my sheep" (John 21:16)
18. Sincerity; truth (1 Corinthians 5:8)
19. The blood of the Lamb (Revelation 7:14)
20. In the Lamb's book of life (Revelation 21:27)

YOUR SCORE: _____

(out of a possible 620 points)
Total number of points from all rounds: _____
Total possible points: 9720

Round 27: Lamb of God/Wrap-up

The sacrifices of lambs without defect, begun in the Old Testament, are a foreshadowing of the ultimate sacrifice of Jesus. Like Abraham, who was poised to sacrifice his only son, Isaac, and the Hebrews who used lamb's blood to prevent the sacrifice of their firstborn sons, God completed the cycle by offering His only Son upon the cross as the *Lamb of God*.

Indeed, as Jesus tells His disciples during their final Passover together on earth, they are to remember Him whenever they partake of the bread and wine. They are to remember His sacrifice for their sins. As believers, whose names will be contained in the Lamb's book of life, we will have the privilege of seeing the Lamb in the new Jerusalem and worshiping Him.

Another port o' call awaits. Round 28 is next.

ROUND 28:
FAITHFUL WITNESS

If you've been playing some kind of game with us for all these rounds, we're ready for the real you—the one with that certain *je ne sais quoi*. Dare we call it by name?

Jesus never failed to provide an accurate picture of Himself throughout His years on earth. That's because He was representing God the Father and because in all things Jesus was and is truthful. In the Book of Revelation, John describes Jesus Christ as "the faithful witness, the firstborn from the dead, and the ruler of the kings of the earth" (Revelation 1:5).

Time to reveal all. It's time to play. . .*Jesus Link!*

ROUND 28:
FAITHFUL WITNESS

Each question in Round 28 is worth 32 points.
Total number of points in this round: 640

 1. In what form did the Spirit of God descend on Jesus during His baptism by John the Baptist?

 2. Complete this sentence about John the Baptist from the Gospel of John: "He himself was not the light; he came only as a ____ to the light."

3. The Gospel writer John says that the law was given through Moses, but ____ and ____ came through Jesus Christ. Complete John's sentence.

 4. Whom did Jesus describe as "a true Israelite, in whom there is nothing false"?

5. Complete Jesus' sentence, recorded in the Book of John: "But whoever lives by the _____ comes into the light, so that it may be seen plainly that what he has done has been done through God."

6. While Jesus says that John the Baptist has "testified to the truth," how does He describe His testimony in relation to John's?

7. Why did Jesus say to the Jewish leaders that the Word of God did not dwell in them, even though they diligently studied the Scriptures?

8. Jesus said that He testifies for Himself, but whom did He say was "my other witness"?

9. To whom was Jesus speaking when He said, "If you hold to my teaching, you are really my disciples"?

10. What nationality were the people who approached Philip after Jesus' triumphal entry into Jerusalem to request an audience with Him?

11. Speaking to that group of people and others, Jesus said that the hour had come for Him to be glorified. To what kind of seed did Jesus compare Himself, illustrating why it was necessary for Him to die?

12. A few sentences later, Jesus cries out, "Father, glorify your name!" What happens immediately afterward?

13. Besides the Counselor, or the Holy Spirit, that Jesus promised to send to testify about Him, whom did Jesus say should testify?

14. Before Jesus ascended into heaven, He told His disciples they would be His witnesses in Jerusalem, in all Judea and Samaria, and where else?

15. To whom is Jesus speaking when He says, "For this reason I was born, and for this I came into the world, to testify to the truth. Everyone on the side of truth listens to me"?

16. Who wrote the following words of wisdom found in the Old Testament: "A truthful witness gives honest testimony, but a false witness tells lies"?

17. After Pentecost, when Peter and other apostles were arrested and put in jail, who set them free during the night?

18. Where were they then told to go, to "tell the people the full message of this new life"?

19. What was the name of the Pharisee who ordered that the apostles not be put to death but rather freed to go their way?

20. Complete this Pharisee's sentence: "Let them go! For if their purpose or activity is of _____ origin, it will fail. But if it is from God, you will not be able to stop these men; you will only find yourselves fighting against God."

ANSWER KEY/ROUND 28: FAITHFUL WITNESS

1. As a dove (Matthew 3:16)
2. "Witness" (John 1:8)
3. Grace; truth (John 1:17)
4. His disciple Nathanael (John 1:47)
5. "Truth" (John 3:21)
6. Jesus' testimony is weightier (John 5:36)
7. Because they didn't believe that Jesus was sent by God (John 5:37–40)
8. His Father (John 8:18)
9. To the Jews who believed Him (John 8:31)
10. They were Greek (John 12:20–21)
11. A kernel of wheat (John 12:24)
12. A thundering voice is heard from heaven saying, "I have glorified it, and will glorify it again" (John 12:28)
13. His believers (John 15:27)
14. To the ends of the earth (Acts 1:8)
15. Pontius Pilate (John 18:37)
16. King Solomon, in the Book of Proverbs (12:17)
17. An angel of the Lord (Acts 5:19)
18. To the temple courts (Acts 5:20)
19. Gamaliel (Acts 5:34)
20. "Human" (Acts 5:38–39)

YOUR SCORE: _____

(out of a possible 640 points)
Total number of points from all rounds: _____
Total possible points: 10,360

Round 28: Faithful Witness/Wrap-up

Jesus was the embodiment of King Solomon's proverb—a truthful witness who could only give honest testimony about Himself. That was the reason He was born on earth. As a *Faithful Witness,* He came to show how, through Him, one might obtain eternal life.

From the dove descending on Him during His baptism to the thundering voice of God proclaiming the glory of His Son, the truth of Jesus' testimony was there for all to see and hear. Today, with the aid of the Holy Spirit, we, too, can be faithful witnesses, proclaiming the truth that is not of human origin but only from God.

Our pace quickens—can we see the barn yet? Round 29 is the penultimate challenge.

ROUND 29:
ALPHA AND OMEGA

"Use your imagination." Sounds like a teacher talking (though probably not one of the Sunday school ilk)—or did you never require such prodding? That dreamy gaze is the first (and last?) sign of a fertile mind!

No human imagination, though, could conceive of Jesus as *Alpha and Omega*, a name based on the first and last letters of the Greek alphabet. Speaking in the Book of Revelation, Jesus says, "I am the Alpha and the Omega. . . who is, and who was, and who is to come, the Almighty" (Revelation 1:8). Jesus, who has already been acknowledged as Creator, or the first, will also be there at the end of the world as we know it. Jesus, who walked the earth as a man, will span the entire history of the universe.

Put your thinking caps on. It's time to play. . .*Jesus Link!*

ROUND 29:
ALPHA AND OMEGA

Each question in Round 29 is worth 33 points.
Total number of points in this round: 660

 1. Who is the "you" in Jesus' statement, "For I tell you, you will not see me again until you say, 'Blessed is he who comes in the name of the Lord' "?

 2. Where must the gospel be preached, according to Jesus, "and then the end will come"?

3. Jesus speaks in great depth about the tribulation period of the end times, that seven-year period that will follow the "rapture" of believers dead and alive. Complete Jesus' sentence: "For then there will be great distress, _____ from the beginning of the world until now."

In the Book of Luke, Jesus compares the evil days prior to His second return to the days of what two Old Testament figures?

5. What did Jesus say were some of the characteristics of Sodom in its final days, according to Luke's Gospel account?

6. Jesus says He will give His believers what two *W* words when we are brought before our adversaries on account of His name?

 Speaking of the tribulation period, Jesus says, "When you see ____ being surrounded by armies, you will know that its desolation is near." Complete Jesus' sentence.

8. When will the "times of the Gentiles" be fulfilled?

 To whom did Jesus say, "I tell you the truth, today you will be with me in paradise"?

The apostle John wrote the Book of Revelation near the end of his life when he was exiled on what island?

 In the third verse of the first chapter of Revelation, whom does John say will receive a blessing?

12. Name three of the seven churches John was directed to write to by Jesus.

13. Complete Jesus' sentence to John: "I am the
_____ _____; I was dead, and behold I am alive for ever and ever! And I hold the keys of death and Hades."

14. In John's vision given by Jesus, who alone is worthy to open the seven seals on the scroll?

 When the seventh seal is opened, what occurs in heaven for "about half an hour"?

16. Following the opening of the seventh seal, what is the next group of seven that appears to John, and what are the members of that group holding?

17. Later John sees seven angels holding seven bowls that contain what, in general?

18. Complete Jesus' sentence to John upon the revealing of the new Jerusalem: "I am the Alpha and the Omega. . . . To him who is _____ I will give to drink without cost from the spring of the water of life."

19. To what precious jewel was the Holy City of Jerusalem compared, when speaking of its brilliance?

20. What five-word sentence is the final one spoken by Jesus to John in the Book of Revelation?

ANSWER KEY/ROUND 29: ALPHA AND OMEGA

1. Jerusalem (Matthew 23:37, 39)
2. In the whole world (Matthew 24:14)
3. "Unequaled" (Matthew 24:21)
4. Noah (Luke 17:26) and Lot (Luke 17:28–29)
5. Eating and drinking; buying and selling; planting and building (Luke 17:28)
6. Words and wisdom (Luke 21:15)
7. "Jerusalem" (Luke 21:20)
8. When the tribulation ends (see Luke 21:24)
9. One of the criminals crucified with Him (Luke 23:43)
10. Patmos (Revelation 1:9)
11. Those who read the words of this prophecy and those who hear it and take to heart what is written
12. Ephesus, Smyrna, Pergamum, Thyatira, Sardis, Philadelphia, and Laodicea (Revelation 1:11)
13. Living One (Revelation 1:18)
14. The Lamb (see Revelation 5)
15. Silence (Revelation 8:1)
16. Seven angels holding seven trumpets (Revelation 8:2)
17. Seven plagues (Revelation 15–16)
18. "Thirsty" (Revelation 21:6)
19. Jasper (Revelation 21:11)
20. "Yes, I am coming soon" (Revelation 22:20)

YOUR SCORE: _____
(out of a possible 660 points)
Total number of points from all rounds: _____
Total possible points: 11,020

ROUND 29: ALPHA AND OMEGA/WRAP-UP

The final days of the world as we know it will be filled with horrible events and evil. Were it not for the return of Jesus Christ, the earth would surely be destroyed. But the good news is that He will return, and this time He will come to reign forever in the new Jerusalem.

Writing on the island of Patmos, the apostle John described in great detail every vision given him by Jesus. But what is most incredible is that Jesus, ever the Good Shepherd, will never leave His believers. He is the *Alpha and Omega,* the First and Last, the Beginning and the End. No force of evil can stand before Him.

Team, prepare for Round 30. The final round will decide it all: Are *you* the *Jesus Link*?

ROUND 30:
SON OF GOD

You've made it to the final round, team, and now 1,000 points are up for grabs. So far you've managed to bag a paltry sum, but there's one last chance to make the *Jesus Link*.

Do you know Jesus as the *Son of God*? Can you make the same declaration as Simon Peter when he acknowledged, "You are the Christ, the Son of the living God" (Matthew 16:16)? That *is* the *Jesus Link*. And that is the hope of John 3:16: "For God so loved the world that he gave his one and only Son, that whoever believes in him shall not perish but have eternal life."

You can't take the walk of shame when you believe that Jesus is the Son of God. It's time to play. . .*Jesus Link!*

Round 30:
Son of God

Each question in Round 30 is worth 50 points.
Total number of points in this round: 1,000

1. Who gave this testimony about Jesus: "No one has ever seen God, but God the One and Only [or only begotten Son], who is at the Father's side, has made him known"?

2. On what day of the week did Jesus heal the invalid man by the pool called Bethesda?

3. To whom did Jesus say, "My Father is always at his work to this very day, and I, too, am working"?

4. Because of this statement, what were two reasons why the Jewish leaders wanted to kill Jesus?

5. What miraculous event preceded Jesus walking on water toward His disciples?

6. Whom did the disciples think Jesus was when they first saw Him on the water?

7. The wind died down when what two men climbed into the disciples' boat?

 8. What did the disciples in the boat say to Jesus when the storm had passed?

9. When Simon Peter declared Jesus to be the Son of the living God, how did Jesus say this had been revealed to Peter?

10. At the Feast of Dedication in Jerusalem, when Jesus told the religious leaders at the temple that He was God's Son, what did they accuse Him of, and what was the punishment?

11. Escaping the religious leaders' grasp, where does Jesus then go, and why did many people begin to believe in Him there?

12. On what occasion did Jesus say, "Father, I thank you that you have heard me. I knew that you always hear me, but I said this for the benefit of the people standing here, that they may believe that you sent me"?

13. Before Jesus performed this miracle, who made this declaration: " 'Yes, Lord,' she told him, 'I believe that you are the Christ, the Son of God, who was to come into the world' "?

14. When did Jesus say, "Father, the time has come. Glorify your Son, that your Son may glorify you"?

15. Who said to Jesus, "What do you want with me, Jesus, Son of the Most High God? I beg you, don't torture me!"?

16. According to the Gospel of Mark, what did evil spirits do whenever they saw Jesus, and what did they say?

17. What did the high priest Caiaphas do after Jesus said, "I am [the Son of the Blessed One]. . .and you will see the Son of Man sitting at the right hand of the Mighty One and coming on the clouds of heaven"?

 18. Who knows the Father, according to Jesus in Luke's Gospel?

19. To whom were the Jewish leaders speaking when they said, "We have a law, and according to that law he must die, because he claimed to be the Son of God"?

 20. When Jesus was baptized by John the Baptist, what did the voice from heaven say?

ANSWER KEY/ROUND 30: SON OF GOD

1. John the Baptist (John 1:18)
2. The Sabbath (John 5:9)
3. The Jews at the temple (John 5:16–17)
4. Because Jesus healed on the Sabbath and because He said that He was God's Son (John 5:18)
5. The feeding of the five thousand (Matthew 14:13–24)
6. A ghost (Matthew 14:26)
7. Jesus and Peter (Matthew 14:29–32)
8. "Truly you are the Son of God" (Matthew 14:33)
9. By His Father in heaven (Matthew 16:17)
10. Blasphemy, a crime punishable by stoning (John 10:33)
11. Across the Jordan River to the place where John the Baptist had been baptizing. People believed in Jesus because all that John said about Him was true (John 10:40–42)
12. The raising of Lazarus from the dead (John 11:41–44)
13. Martha, Lazarus's sister (John 11:24–27)
14. The time of His betrayal, crucifixion, and Resurrection (see John 17–18)
15. The demon-possessed man who lived in the tombs (Luke 8:27–28)
16. Evil spirits fell down and cried out, "You are the Son of God" (Mark 3:11)
17. He tore his clothes (Mark 14:62–63)
18. The Son and those to whom the Son chooses to reveal the Father (Luke 10:22)
19. Pontius Pilate (John 19:6–7)
20. "This is my Son, whom I love; with him I am well pleased" (Matthew 3:17)

YOUR SCORE: _____
(out of a possible 1,000 points)
Total number of points from all rounds: _____
Total possible points: 12,020

Round 30: Son of God/Wrap-up

Jesus, though He appeared on earth as a "mere man," according to the religious leaders of the temple, was God's only Son in the flesh—a fact acknowledged by even the demons of the evil one! Only He was given the power to perform miracles never before seen; only He was given the ability to forgive sins and offer eternal life as the reward for believing in Him.

For that, He was sentenced to die upon the cross—an ending, but yet the beginning that was all part of the plan to glorify Jesus and bring generations to believe in Him. The apostle John writes, "The Father loves the Son and has placed everything in his hands. Whoever believes in the Son has eternal life, but whoever rejects the Son will not see life, for God's wrath remains on him" (John 3:35–36).

To you who have encountered thirty names of Jesus and delved into your memory banks of Scripture to find the answers to some of the most particular questions ever posed. . .you *are* the *Jesus Link!* Good-bye!

ABOUT THE AUTHOR

ELLEN CAUGHEY is a freelance writer and editor in New Jersey. She has written a number of books for Barbour Publishing, including Heroes of the Faith biographies of Eric Liddell, Charles Sheldon, and John Wycliffe.